CityPack
Boston

BY SUE GORDON

When Sue Gordon spent the summer of 1963 living with a Boston family, she little knew that three decades later she would be co-authoring the AA Explorer guide, Boston & New England. *A freelance writer and editor, she returns at every opportunity, taking particular delight in directing her Bostonian friends to corners of their city that they have never visited.*

City-centre map continues on inside back cover

AA Publishing

Contents

life 5–12

INTRODUCING BOSTON 6–8
BOSTON IN FIGURES 9
A CHRONOLOGY 10–11

PEOPLE & EVENTS
FROM HISTORY 12

how to organise your time 13–22

ITINERARIES 14–15
WALKS 16–17
EVENING STROLLS 18
ORGANISED SIGHTSEEING 19

EXCURSIONS 20–21
WHAT'S ON 22

top 25 sights 23–48

1 LONGFELLOW HOUSE &
   BRATTLE STREET 24
2 HARVARD SQUARE &
   HARVARD UNIVERSITY 25
3 HARVARD UNIVERSITY
   MUSEUMS 26
4 ISABELLA STEWART
   GARDNER MUSEUM 27
5 MUSEUM OF FINE ARTS 28
6 FIRST CHURCH OF CHRIST,
   SCIENTIST 29
7 PRUDENTIAL & HANCOCK
   TOWERS 30
8 BOSTON PUBLIC LIBRARY 31
9 TRINITY CHURCH 32
10 BACK BAY &
   COMMONWEALTH AVENUE 33
11 MUSEUM OF SCIENCE 34
12 BEACON HILL &
   LOUISBURG SQUARE 35
13 BOSTON COMMON & THE
   PUBLIC GARDEN 36

14 HARRISON GRAY
   OTIS HOUSE 37
15 MASSACHUSETTS STATE
   HOUSE 38
16 BEACON STREET &
   THE ATHENAEUM 39
17 OLD SOUTH MEETING
   HOUSE 40
18 OLD STATE HOUSE 41
19 FANEUIL HALL &
   MARKETPLACE 42
20 USS *CONSTITUTION* &
   CHARLESTOWN 43
21 THE NORTH END & OLD
   NORTH CHURCH 44
22 PAUL REVERE HOUSE 45
23 NEW ENGLAND AQUARIUM 46
24 BOSTON HARBOR ISLANDS 47
25 JOHN F KENNEDY LIBRARY
   & MUSEUM 48

Index 94–95

About this book 4

best 49–60

Neighbourhoods | 50–51
Houses, Museums & Galleries | 52–53
Buildings: Late 19th & 20th Century | 54
Statues, Monuments & Sculptures | 55

Places of Worship & Burial Grounds | 56
Parks & Retreats | 57
Sports & Outdoor Activities | 58
Things for Children to See & Do | 59
Freebies & Cheapies | 60

where to... 61–86

EAT

The Best of Boston | 62–63
Seafood | 64
Italian & Mediterranean | 65
American & Mexican | 66
Asian & Middle Eastern | 67
Brunch, Coffee, Tea & Late Eating | 68–69

SHOP

Districts & Department Stores | 70–71
Clothes | 72–73
Shoes & Outdoor Gear | 74

Books, Maps & Music | 75
Crafts, Gifts & Household Goods | 76–77

BE ENTERTAINED

Classical Music, Opera & Dance | 78–79
Theatre & Cinema | 80–81
Clubs & Bars | 82–83

STAY

Luxury Hotels | 84
Mid-Range Hotels | 85
Budget Accommodation | 86

travel facts 87–93

Arriving & Departing | 88–89
Essential Facts | 89–91
Public Transport | 91–92
Driving & Car Hire | 92–93

Media & Communications | 93
Emergencies | 93

Credits, Acknowledgements and Titles in This Series | 96

About this book

KEY TO SYMBOLS

✚	map reference on the fold-out map accompanying this book (see below)	🚌	nearest bus route
✉	address	🚢	nearest riverboat or ferry stop
☎	telephone number	♿	facilities for visitors with disabilities
🕐	opening times	✋	admission charge
🍴	restaurant or café on premises or nearby	↔	other nearby places of interest
Ⓜ	nearest T (underground) subway station	❓	tours, lectures or special events
🚉	nearest railway station	►	indicates the page where you will find a fuller description
		ℹ	tourist information

CityPack Boston is divided into six sections to cover the six most important aspects of your visit to Boston. It includes:

- The author's view of the city and its people
- Itineraries, walks and excursions
- The top 25 sights to visit – as selected by the author
- Features about different aspects of the city that make it special
- Detailed listings of restaurants, hotels, shops and nightlife
- Practical information

In addition, easy-to-read side panels provide fascinating extra facts and snippets, highlights of places to visit and invaluable practical advice.

CROSS-REFERENCES

To help you make the most of your visit, cross-references, indicated by ► , show you where to find additional information about a place or subject.

MAPS

The fold-out map in the wallet at the back of the book is a comprehensive street plan of Boston. All the map references given in the book refer to this map. For example, Trinity Church on Copley Square has the following information: ✚ F5 – indicating the grid square of the map in which Trinity Church will be found.

The city map found on the inside front and back covers of the book itself is for quick reference. It shows the top 25 sights in the city, described on pages 24–48, which are clearly plotted by number (**1**–**25**, not page number) from west to east.

ADMISSION CHARGES

An indication of the admission charge for museums and galleries is given by categorising the standard adult rate as follows: expensive (over $7), moderate ($4–$6) and inexpensive (under $4).

BOSTON
life

Introducing Boston   6–8

Boston in Figures   9

A Chronology   10–11

*People & Events from
History*   12

INTRODUCING BOSTON

The Proper Bostonian

The Brahmins, or Proper Bostonians, trace their origins to the wealthy merchants of the 18th and 19th centuries. Membership of these families – names such as Lowell, Appleton, Cabot – may now be comparatively minimal, but their influence is still felt.

'And this is the city of Boston
The land of the bean and the cod
Where the Lowells talk only to
Cabots
And the Cabots talk only to God'.

Toast made by James Collins Bassidy, Alumni dinner at Holy Cross College, 1910

Boston has changed not only in size but also – radically – in shape since the 1620s, when a group of early British colonists chose this spot on which to build their life. Boston is still a place blessed in its location, with the sea and all its pleasures lapping at the front door, the sweeping Charles River at the side entrance and forests and mountains in its back garden.

But what of the city itself? Its history – and there simply is no other American city that has such a long history – is deeply revered and meticulously preserved. Its role as the cradle of the nation and the birthplace of the American Revolution is vividly interpreted in various landmarks along the Freedom Trail, a red line on the sidewalk that guides you from one significant site to the next. In the 19th century wealthy Bostonians (and there were many) travelled extensively in Europe, leaving their city an exceptional cultural legacy that is now displayed in such nationally and internationally important treasure houses as the Museum of Fine Arts, the Isabella Stewart Gardner Museum and Harvard's Fogg Museum.

As for the architecture, one of the most exciting things about Boston are the unexpected juxtapositions of elegant old and high-rise new, not least the Hancock Tower, a gleaming shaft of glass, which at every turn, it seems, rises serene above Victorian brownstone rooftops. Musically, the city is home not only to the world-class Boston Symphony Orchestra, but also the Boston Pops, seriously good jazz and some hip rock bands. The boutiques and stores in the old Victorian brownstone houses of Newbury Street, one of the most inviting in the country, together with a clutch of malls, make for exceptional shopping.

Boston may have one eye gazing at the past, but the other is firmly fixed on the future. Across the river is Cambridge, home of Harvard and MIT (Massachusetts Institute of

Charles Street storefront

Technology), and between them, Boston and Cambridge boast over 60 colleges and universities. Not surprisingly, life in 'the Hub' has a certain intellectual edge. The 100,000 students give the place a buzz. The international ones among them, together with the city's ethnic population, add a certain diversity, which is reflected in a spirited, ever-burgeoning restaurant scene.

Trinity Church reflected in the glass of the Hancock Tower

7

*Alfresco dining on
Newbury Street*

The Big Dig

Boston's one major blight
currently is the 'Big Dig', an epic
roadworks project that will take
until 2004 to put below ground
the elevated expressway, the
Central Artery. Once buried, it will
be covered with parkland,
reuniting with downtown Boston
the North End and the Waterfront
that currently can only be reached
by picking your way (as sign-
posted) through the roadworks.

Traditionally, Bostonians were regarded by other
Americans as snobby, sedate, a little behind the
times – a legacy of the Brahmins, as the city's rich
and powerful upper-caste establishment was
termed in the 19th century. And on elitist
Beacon Hill, you may still get a sense of what
that was all about. But nowadays what impresses
the visitor most is the fact that the city is not only
one of the most attractive in the country but also
one of the easiest to explore. The historic core is
compact, and can be explored in a leisurely day
or two. Whether you are doing the sights, attend-
ing a conference or having a shopping spree, easy
footwork will get you most places. If you do tire
of walking, want to conserve energy for the
Fenway galleries or plan to venture over the
river to Harvard Square in Cambridge, there is
always the T, as the underground is called, which
is cheap, clean, efficient and simple to use.

And what is it like, living in Boston? In the city
of high-rise finance and high-tech research, the
city of the Red Sox and the Celtics, Filene's
Basement and Dunkin' Donuts, Italian *feste* and
Irish politicians (Democrat or Democrat?)
Bostonians work hard, but they also play hard. If
you are up early, you'll see professionals hustling
along in their trainers and sharp suits, styrofoam
cup of coffee in one hand, a bagel in a bag in the
other. Supper is eaten early, and then there's the
evening entertainment – maybe a game at
Fenway Park (you never know, the Red Sox just
might make it this season), a concert at
Symphony Hall, a foreign film, a meal in South
End. Saturday sees many Bostonians shopping
in the North End's Italian groceries, jogging on
the Esplanade or taking the children to the
Aquarium. Sundays could mean a stroll through
Back Bay Fens, brunch and an afternoon concert
at the Gardner Museum or perhaps the family
might head for one of the Boston Harbor Islands
for the day. For holidays, there may be a trip to
Maine or Cape Cod, and in winter there's skiing
in the Berkshires, Vermont or New Hampshire.
There is so much choice for Bostonians. Their
17th-century forebears chose well.

BOSTON IN FIGURES

Population
- 1690: 7,000
- 1790: 18,320
- 1825: 58,277
- 1850: 136,881
- 1875: 341,919
- 1996: 574,283

Topography
- Area of central Boston: 48.6 square miles
- 58 per cent is landfill, including Back Bay, South End, South Boston
- 43 miles of waterfront
- Beacon Hill was one of three peaks called Trimountaine by early colonists

Nicknames
- The Hub: in 1858 Oliver Wendell Holmes, essayist and lecturer, called the Massachusetts State House 'the hub of the solar system'; now applied to Boston as a whole
- Beantown: as it was against the law for the Puritans to cook on Sunday, they prepared baked beans on Saturdays. This custom earned Boston the nickname Beantown
- Athens of America: expression used by William Tudor in 1819
- Brahmin: term coined by Oliver Wendell Holmes after the high-ranking Hindu caste
- Proper Bostonians (▶ 6)
- 'Old Ironsides': USS *Constitution*, because her wooden hull survived many attacks
- The T: rapid transport system (underground)

Boston & Cambridge academia
- 67 colleges and universities
- 100,000 students
- 8 major medical research centres
- Half the population of Cambridge is connected with academic institutions

Boston firsts
- Boston Common, first park in US: 1634
- *Boston News Letter*, first newspaper in US: 1704
- Alexander Graham Bell makes first telephone call: 1875
- The first subway in the Western hemisphere opens under Boston Common: 1897
- First kidney transplant: 1954

A CHRONOLOGY

Pre-1620	The Boston area is inhabited by the Massachusetts Algonquins.
1620	Pilgrims arrive on *Mayflower* and establish first English colony in Plymouth.
1624	Clergyman William Blaxton settles on what is now Beacon Hill on the Shawmut peninsula.
1629	Puritans found Massachusetts Bay Colony in Charlestown.
1630	John Winthrop becomes first governor and Colony moves to Shawmut peninsula.
1636	Harvard College is founded to train ministers.
1680	The house that Paul Revere was to live in a century later is built. Most of Boston is concentrated in what is to become the North End, around the flourishing seaport.
1760s	Britain imposes a series of tax-levying acts. Colonists protest at having to pay taxes when they have no representation in government. Tension mounts. Patriots are led by 'Sons of Freedom' Sam Adams and John Hancock.
1770	March 5: British soldiers kill five colonists outside the State House ('Boston Massacre').
1773	December 16: Patriots protest at the Tea Act by throwing tea into the sea (Boston Tea Party).
1775	The Revolution starts in Boston.
1776	March 17: British leave Boston. July 18: Declaration of Independence read from State House balcony.
1799–1805	Beacon Hill is pared down by some 60ft.
1790s	China trade prosperity.
1795	Architect Charles Bulfinch (▶ 12) starts new State House.

1800	The Mount Vernon Proprietors (including Bulfinch) develop Beacon Hill.
1826	Mayor Josiah Quincy extends waterfront and builds Quincy Market.
1840s	Irish immigrants, fleeing the potato famine, pour into the North End.
1856	Work begins on filling in and developing the Back Bay as a new residential area for the elite.
1877	Swan boats come to the Public Garden.
1880s	Irish make their mark in politics; Irish mayors include John F Fitzgerald ('Honey-Fitz'), grandfather of John F Kennedy, and the charismatic James Curley.
1895	Frederick Law Olmsted, Boston's first landscape architect, designs an interconnecting chain of parks, 'The Emerald Necklace'.
1897	First Boston Marathon takes place.
1918	Red Sox win the World Series – their first and only baseball victory.
1928	Boston Garden opens. It closes on 29 September 1995.
1957	First of 16 NBA championship victories by the Celtics.
1960	John F Kennedy (► 12) elected President.
1960s–70s	An extensive urban renewal programme includes John Hancock Tower.
1989	Work begins on burying the Central Artery (► 8).
1990	Art robbery at the Stewart Gardner Museum.
2000	Boston is one of eight international Tall Ships 2000 ports.

PEOPLE & EVENTS FROM HISTORY

Tea is thrown overboard in protest against the British tax on tea – a significant event in the build up to revolution

Charles Bulfinch

It is often said that Charles Bulfinch (1763–1844) more or less made Boston architecturally. Returning from a trip to Europe, he designed a new State House and a dozen churches. He then turned to the large-scale residential development of Beacon Hill. His neoclassical style became known as 'Federal'. Having made his mark in Boston, Bulfinch went on to design the Capitol in Washington, DC.

THE BOSTON TEA PARTY

By the mid-1700s the New England colonists were feeling increasingly angry at British interference in their lucrative seafaring trade. In 1773 the Tea Act not only levied a tax but gave London's East India Company a monopoly on the tea trade. Tension mounted and, in December, patriots took decisive action by boarding three of the company's ships in the harbour and dumping the tea overboard. The British retaliated by besieging Boston, and war became inevitable.

PAUL REVERE'S RIDE

In his lifetime Revere (1735–1818) was known principally as a silversmith. He was also involved in the pre-Revolutionary activities of the 'Sons of Liberty' and acted as a messenger to warn local militia men about British military preparations. On the night of 18 April 1775, as a signal to patriots in Charlestown that the troops were leaving, he arranged for lanterns to be hung in the steeple of Old North Church. He then left for Concord himself but, with William Dawes and Sam Prescott, was captured by the British. Only Prescott escaped. Most press reports did not even mention Revere by name. However, in 1861 Longfellow was inspired to pen a poem. He used poetic license: Revere receives rather than gives the signal; Revere not only rides to Concord alone, he arrives safely. And thus, Revere the folk hero is immortalised.

JFK

John Fitzgerald Kennedy was born in the Boston suburb of Brookline on 29 May 1917 into a politically active Irish-American family. A Harvard graduate, he served in the navy in World War II and in 1946 was elected to Congress from Boston. From 1953 to 1960 he served in the US Senate. He was elected president in 1960. Good-looking and charismatic, with a beautiful and equally charismatic wife, he was a symbol of the nation's hopes for a progressive future. Tragically, on 22 November 1963, he was assassinated in Dallas.

BOSTON
how to organise your time

ITINERARIES   14–15
  On and off the Freedom Trail
  Beacon Hill & Back Bay
  Culture in Fenway
  A day in Cambridge

WALKS   16–17
  Beacon Hill
  The Freedom Trail to Copp's Hill

EVENING STROLLS   18
  Faneuil & the Waterfront
  The Charles River & Back Bay
  Harvard Square

ORGANISED SIGHTSEEING   19

EXCURSIONS   20–21
  Concord
  Lowell
  Salem
  Plymouth

WHAT'S ON   22

ITINERARIES

| ITINERARY ONE | ON AND OFF THE FREEDOM TRAIL |

Morning

Massachusetts State House (► 38). Bowdoin Street, Derne Street, Hancock Street to Harrison Gray Otis House (► 37). Cambridge Street, Bowdoin Street, Beacon Street.

Lunch

Black Goose ✉ 21 Beacon Street.

Afternoon

Park Street, then Tremont Street for Old Granary Burying Ground (► 56) and King's Chapel (► 56).
Keep on trail to Old South Meeting House (► 40), Old State House (► 41) and Faneuil Hall (► 42). Refreshment in Faneuil Hall Marketplace. Continue on trail to Paul Revere House (► 45) and Old North Church, North End (► 44). If time, USS *Constitution* (► 43).

Evening

Meal in the North End (► 65).

| ITINERARY TWO | BEACON HILL & BACK BAY |

Morning

Start at Park T. Walk up Park Street and left down Beacon Street. Right onto Charles Street to explore Beacon Hill (► 16, 35).
Coffee on Charles Street. Try Rebecca's Bakery (► 68).
Public Garden (► 36) to Washington Statue and onto Commonwealth Avenue (► 33). Left onto Fairfield Street. Cross Boylston Street to Prudential Center (► 30, 71).

Lunch

Legal Sea Foods (► 64).

Afternoon

Walk through Prudential Center to First Church of Christ, Scientist for Mapparium (► 29). Return through Prudential Center and covered walk to Copley Place. Exit onto Dartmouth Street.
Copley Square for Boston Public Library (► 31) and Trinity Church (► 32), or tea or a drink at Fairmount Copley Plaza Hotel (► 84).

Evening

John Hancock Tower Observatory (► 30). Meal in Newbury Street or Boylston Street.

ITINERARY THREE	**CULTURE IN FENWAY**
Morning	T to the Museum of Fine Arts (➤ 28), taking refreshment when necessary in one of the museum's cafés.
Lunch	The Museum of Fine Arts (choice of restaurants) or around the corner in Isabella Stewart Gardner Museum Café.
Afternoon	Isabella Stewart Gardner Museum (➤ 27). Through Back Bay Fens to Boylston Street.
Evening	Drink or meal at Sonsie (➤ 69). Prudential Skywalk (➤ 30).
ITINERARY FOUR	**CAMBRIDGE**
Morning	T to Harvard Square for coffee. With Harvard Coop on your left and the newspaper stall on your right, walk up Massachusetts Avenue to the First Church Burial Ground. Cross Massachusetts Avenue and Peabody Street to enter Harvard Yard (➤ 25). Walk through to Quincy Street for the Fogg Art Museum and Busch-Reisinger (➤ 26). Follow Quincy Street to Sackler Museum (➤ 26). If you wish to see the Glass Flowers (➤ 26), continue on Quincy Street across Cambridge Street. Left on Kirkland Street, right onto Oxford Street. Retrace steps to corner of Oxford and Kirkland streets and return through Harvard Yard to Harvard Square.
Lunch	Choice in Brattle Street.
Afternoon	Continue westward on Brattle Street. Opposite American Repertory Theatre, divert right to see Radcliffe Yard (➤ 25). Brattle Street to Longfellow House (➤ 24). Walk through the park in front of Longfellow House. Turn left on Mount Auburn Street to return to Harvard Square.
Evening	Casablanca (➤ 67) or House of Blues (➤ 68).

WALKS

Louisburg Square

THE SIGHTS

- Beacon Hill (➤ 35)
- Nichols House (➤ 53)
- African Meeting House (➤ 53)

INFORMATION

Distance 1½ miles
Time 1 hour
Start point Beacon Street (by State House)
⊞ bIV; B4
🚇 Park
End point Beacon Street at Charles Street
⊞ bIV; B4
🚇 Park

BEACON HILL

Beacon Hill is steep in parts and some of the streets are cobbled. Wear suitable shoes.

Start on Beacon Street at the State House and walk downhill. The Appleton Mansions at No. 39, where poet Longfellow was married, and No. 40 have some of the highly prized purple panes (flawed originals that are now rare ➤ 35). At the bottom turn right onto Charles Street, up Chestnut Street and left onto Willow Street. On the left is a much-photographed view down Acorn Street. Houses in lanes such as this were for servants. Continue to Mount Vernon Street. The beautiful Louisburg Square, where author Louisa May Alcott died, is ahead. Continue up Mt Vernon Street and detour onto Walnut Street and briefly into Chestnut to see Nos. 13, 15 and 17, a lovely trio. Return to Mt. Vernon Street to visit the Nichols House, a family home until the 1960s. At the end of Mt Vernon, turn left onto Joy Street. Smith Court, important in the history of African Americans in Boston, is farther down Joy Street, over Pinckney Street. Turn onto Pinckney Street, with its fine view of the Charles River. Detour right onto Anderson Street and right again onto Revere Street. Between 29 and 25 the columned façade is a *trompe l'oeil*. Return to Pinckney and follow it down to Charles Street.

Return to Beacon Street. From here you can join the Freedom Trail in front of the State House.

THE FREEDOM TRAIL TO COPP'S HILL

The Freedom Trail is a long-established walking tour that links all the most significant sites from Boston's colonial and revolutionary era. A red line (painted or brick) on the sidewalk makes it easy to follow.

Start at the information centre on Boston Common. Head for the classical gold-domed Massachusetts State House. Facing it is the Shaw Monument. Come down Park Street to 'Brimstone Corner' (gunpowder was stored in Park Street Church in the war of 1812) and turn left onto Tremont Street. Many famous people are buried in the Old Granary Burying Ground. Cross to King's Chapel, the oldest church site in Boston still in use. Turn down School Street. A pavement mosaic marks the site of the first free school, open to all. On the left, in front of the Old City Hall, is a statue of Benjamin Franklin. At the end of the street, the Old Corner Bookstore was a meeting place for 19th-century literati. Head diagonally right past a sculpture of Irish potato famine immigrants for Old South Meeting House, where the Boston Tea Party started. Follow the red line along Washington Street to Old State House. A circle of stones in the traffic island on State Street marks the site of the Boston Massacre. Cross State Street onto Congress Street. Faneuil Hall and Marketplace (plenty of eating places here) is on the right.

Continue along the trail between the tall glass Holocaust Memorial and the Olde Union Oyster House to Hanover Street. Cross Blackstone Street and follow the signed walkway under the Expressway to the North End. Turn right off Hanover Street onto Richmond Steet for North Square and Paul Revere's House. Back in Hanover Street, turn left onto Revere Mall, passing Revere's statue, with the landmark of Old North Church steeple ahead. Carry on up Hull Street for Copp's Hill Burying Ground.

THE SIGHTS

- State House (➤ 38)
- Shaw Monument (➤ 55)
- Park Street Church (➤ 56)
- Old Granary Burying Ground (➤ 56)
- King's Chapel (➤ 56)
- Old South Meeting House (➤ 40)
- Old State House (➤ 41)
- Faneuil Hall (➤ 42)
- Holocaust Memorial (➤ 55)
- Paul Revere House (➤ 45)
- St Stephen's Church (➤ 56)
- Old North Church (➤ 44)
- Copp's Hill Burying Ground (➤ 56)

INFORMATION

Distance 1½ miles
Time 1–4 hours
Start point Boston Common
➕ blV; B4
🚇 Park
End point Copp's Hill
➕ dl; H3
🚇 North station

John Hancock's tombstone, Old Granary Burying Ground

17

EVENING STROLLS

Faneuil Hall and Marketplace

FANEUIL HALL & THE WATERFRONT

For superb views of the city and harbour, start with a drink in the Bay Tower, 60 State Street (jacket and tie). Stroll through Faneuil Hall Marketplace, a lively collection of shops and eating places, then follow the Harborwalk across Atlantic Avenue and south along the old wharves of the Waterfront. At the old Northern Avenue Bridge, walk right of James Hook's lobster shed, then turn left to go over New Northern Avenue Bridge. Look right – up Fort Point Channel – and see the Boston Tea Party Ship, a replica of one of the original ships, silhouetted against the evening sky. End up at one of the seafood restaurants in the vicinity (▶ 64).

THE CHARLES RIVER & BACK BAY

From the western edge of the always delightful Public Garden, cross Arlington Street and walk through Commonwealth Avenue's central gardens. At Dartmouth Street turn right and take a footbridge that leads you to the Esplanade, beside the river. Walk left past pretty Storrow Lagoon to a footbridge that takes you onto Fairfield Street. Turn left onto Newbury Street as far as Dartmouth Street. Turn right onto Copley Square. Have a drink in the Fairmount Copley Plaza Hotel, noting the sumptuous decor, then visit the Hancock Tower Observatory for magical night-time views before or after eating at Skipjack's (▶ 64), Café Budapest (▶ 62) or in the South End (▶ 63).

HARVARD SQUARE

Harvard Square – its shops, restaurants, bars and clubs – is awake till the small hours. Stroll around the streets imbibing the atmosphere (or if you are a book lover, just browse to your heart's content), then choose a restaurant or retreat to the Charles Hotel's Regatta Bar Jazz Club.

INFORMATION

Faneuil Hall & the Waterfront
Distance 1¼–1½ miles
Time 40 minutes
Start point 60 State Street
✚ dlll; H4
🚇 State
End point Northern Avenue
✚ H5
🚇 South station

Charles River & Back Bay
Distance 1¼ miles
Time 30–40 minutes
Start point Public Garden
✚ F5
🚇 Arlington
End point Copley Square
✚ F5
🚇 Copley

Harvard Square
Start/end point Harvard Square
✚ C2
🚇 Harvard Square

Organised Sightseeing

ON FOOT

Black Heritage Trail Explores the history of the African-American community on Beacon Hill ✉ Museum of Afro-American History, 46 Joy Street ☎ 617/742 1854.
Boston by Foot Range of tours for all ages ✉ 77 North Washington Street ☎ 617/367 2345 🕙 May–Oct.
Freedom Trail Ranger-led tours that connect the city's historic sites (► 17) ✉ Visitor Center, 15 State Street ☎ 617/242 5642 🕙 Spring–autumn: daily 🎟 Free.
North End Market Tours (► 77, panel).

TROLLEY TOURS

All do narrated tours, stopping at major sites, shopping districts and principal hotels. All also do tours of Cambridge. Hop and off all day ticket 🕙 Daily from 9AM. **Beantown Trolley** (red) ☎ 617/236 2148 or 800/343 1328 takes in Museum of Fine Arts. **Minuteman Trolley Tours** (blue) ☎ 617/269 3626. **Old Town Trolleys** (green and orange) ☎ 617/269 7010. **Discover Boston Multi-Lingual Trolley Tours** ☎ 617/742 1440.

DUCK TOURS

Boston Duck Tours Renovated World War II amphibious vehicles tour historic Boston and then splash into the Charles River. Tours leave half-hourly, from Prudential Center, Huntington Avenue side. Expect a long queue for tickets ☎ 617/723 DUCK 🕙 Apr–Nov: daily.

WHALEWATCHING AND BOAT TOURS

Aquarium Whalewatch trips (► 46).
Boston Harbor Cruises Whalewatch trips, sightseeing cruises, sunset cruises, George's Island ferry ✉ 1 Long Wharf ☎ 617/227 4321 🕙 Daily.
Boston Tall Ships Sail in an 18th-century fishing schooner replica ✉ 50 Rowes Wharf ☎ 617/742 0333 🕙 Jun–Sep.
Charles River Boat Company River cruises ✉ CambridgeSide Place ☎ 617/621 3001 🕙 Memorial Day–Labor Day: daily. Apr, May, Oct: Sat, Sun only.
Massachusetts Bay Lines Historical harbour tours, cruises, whalewatch trips ✉ Rowes Wharf ☎ 617/542 8000 🕙 May–Oct.

Out of Boston Tours

Brush Hill Tours/Gray Line ☎ 617/236 2148 or 800/343 1328 operate tours to Cambridge/Lexington/Concord, Plimoth Plantation and Plymouth Rock, Salem, Newport, Cape Cod. Pick up from major Boston and Cambridge hotels.

Bostonian trolley bus

Excursions

An excursion out of Boston gives you the chance to see some New England countryside, not to mention all those picture-postcard clapboard houses. The places described below are easily accessible by public transport. Train schedules are available at some T stations. If you have a car, you could make a combined trip to Concord and Lowell.

INFORMATION

Concord

Distance About 20 miles

Journey time 40 minutes

⊙ Emerson's and Hawthorne's houses closed winter; other sites open all year, hours vary

🚉 T trains from North station

ℹ Greater Merrimack Valley Visitors Bureau

✉ 22 Shattuck Street, Lowell, MA 01852

☎ 800/433 3332

Lowell

Distance About 30 miles

Journey time 45 minutes

⊙ Boott Mills open daily; Quilt Museum, Sports Museum closed Mon; Whistler House closed Mon, Tue and Jan–Feb

🚉 T trains from North station, then shuttle bus to downtown

ℹ Market Mills Visitor Center

✉ 246 Market Street, Lowell, MA 01852 ☎ 978/459 1062

❓ Reservations needed for canal/trolley tours ☎ 978/ 970 5017

CONCORD

A lot of history is packed into Concord – a small, pretty town with pleasant shops and places to eat and stay. In Revolutionary Concord, the key point is the North Bridge (¾ mile from the centre of town), where on 19 April 1775, the first battle in the Revolution took place. This is commemorated by Daniel Chester French's *Minute Man* statue. There is also Literary Concord: in the 19th century an influential group of writers and transcendentalist thinkers lived here including Nathaniel Hawthorne, Louisa May Alcott and her father Bronson, Ralph Waldo Emerson and Henry Thoreau. Their houses are open to the public (some seasonally). All are buried in Sleepy Hollow Cemetery. The Concord Museum draws the threads together, with exhibits such as one of the two lanterns that were hung in the steeple of Old North Church as a signal to the patriots, and a recreation of Emerson's study.

LOWELL

Anyone with an interest in industrial archaeology or textiles will appreciate Lowell, the town where the Industrial Revolution began in the USA. A highly acclaimed urban regeneration scheme has restored many cotton

Minute Man, *Concord*

mills and 5½ miles of canals. In summer, visitors tour this National Historical Park area of the town by canal boat and trolley, in winter by ranger-led and self-guided walk. The Market Mills Visitor Center gives a good introduction and is the starting point for tours. In Boott Cotton Mills Museum the weave room has 88 looms in operation (free ear-plugs are supplied) and the Working People Exhibit, in former mill-workers' housing, gives a good picture of the life led by the workers. Lowell also has a quilt museum, Whistler House (birthplace of artist James McNeill Whistler), and the Sports Museum of New England.

SALEM

To most people Salem means first and foremost witches. The town certainly makes the most of it, with a range of interpretations of the mass hysteria of the 1690s. The best of the bunch is the Salem Witch Museum. However, the town also has a particularly rich maritime history and, resulting from it, some of the best Federal architecture in America. In the 18th and early 19th centuries Salem's prosperous ship builders, sea captains and merchants built graceful houses and filled them with beautiful things. Many of these objects are now in the Peabody Essex Museum, a vast collection of Far Eastern decorative arts, furniture, maritime painting and Native and Early American artefacts.

PLYMOUTH

The landing of the Pilgrims in 1620 (the exact location is debated) is commemorated on the town's waterfront by Plymouth Rock. Docked next to it is the replica *Mayflower II*, which visitors can board. Three miles south is Plimoth Plantation, a meticulously accurate reproduction of the Pilgrims' settlement as it was in 1627. As on *Mayflower II*, 'interpreters' in period costume faithfully act out the parts, chatting with visitors while getting on with daily chores. At the Wampanoag Indian Homesite, Native Americans, on whose ancestors' land the Pilgrims settled, tell of their experiences.

Peabody Museum, Salem

INFORMATION

Salem
Distance About 16 miles
Journey time 30 minutes
- 🕐 Peabody Essex Museum closed Mon in winter. Witch Museum open daily
- 🚆 T trains from North station
- 🚌 From Boston, call tourist office
- ℹ️ Destination Salem ✉ 10 Liberty Street, Salem ☎ 877/725 3662

Plymouth
Distance About 50 miles
Journey time About 1 hour
- ☎ Plimoth Plantation 508/746 1622
- 🕐 Mayflower II and Plimoth Plantation Apr–Nov
- 🚆 Trains from South station
- ℹ️ Destination Plymouth ✉ 225 Water Street, Plymouth ☎ 800/872 1620

21

WHAT'S ON

January	*Martin Luther King weekend.*
February	*Chinese New Year* (Jan/Feb).
March	*Spring Flower Show* (mid-month). *St Patrick's Day Parade.*
April	*Patriots Day* (3rd Mon) Revere's Ride re-created. *Boston Marathon* (3rd Mon). *Kite Festival* (or May): Franklin Park.
May	*Harvard Square Book Festival.* *Boston Pops Concerts*: Season starts early May.
June	*Battle of Bunker Hill re-enactment*: (Sunday before Bunker Hill Day, 17 Jun). *Harborlights Music Festival* (Jun–Sep): Waterfront concerts. *Boston Globe Jazz Festival*: Various locations.
July	*Boston Pops Concerts*: Free outdoor concerts. *Independence celebrations* (week of 4 Jul): Boston Pops concert with fireworks, Boston Harborfest music festival, and USS *Constitution* turnaround. *Italian feste* (street festivals, Jul/Aug weekends): In the North End.
August	*Moon Festival*: Processions in Chinatown.
September	*Cambridge River Festival*: Events on the river.
October	*Columbus Day Parade.* *Head of the Charles Regatta* (3rd week). *Boston Symphony Orchestra*: Season Oct–Apr.
November	*Christmas tree lighting ceremonies*: Faneuil Marketplace and Charles Square, Cambridge. *Boston Ballet*: *The Nutcracker* (Nov–Dec): Wang Center.
December	*Tree lighting ceremonies*: Prudential Center, Harvard Square. *Boston Tea Party* (mid-Dec): Re-enactment. *Carol concert*: Trinity Church, Copley Square. *New Year's Eve*: First Night celebrations.

BOSTON's
top 25 sights

The sights are numbered **1–25** *from west to east across the city*

1 *Longfellow House &*
Brattle Street 24
2 *Harvard Square &*
Harvard University 25
3 *Harvard University*
Museums 26
4 *Isabella Stewart Gardner*
Museum 27
5 *Museum of Fine Arts* 28
6 *First Church of Christ,*
Scientist 29
7 *Prudential & Hancock*
Towers 30
8 *Boston Public Library* 31
9 *Trinity Church* 32
10 *Back Bay & Commonwealth*
Avenue 33
11 *Museum of Science* 34
12 *Beacon Hill & Louisburg*
Square 35

13 *Boston Common &*
The Public Garden 36
14 *Harrison Gray Otis House* 37
15 *Massachusetts State House* 38
16 *Beacon Street & The*
Athenaeum 39
17 *Old South Meeting House* 40
18 *Old State House* 41
19 *Faneuil Hall &*
Marketplace 42
20 *USS* Constitution *&*
Charlestown 43
21 *The North End & Old*
North Church 44
22 *Paul Revere House* 45
23 *New England Aquarium* 46
24 *Boston Harbor Islands* 47
25 *John F Kennedy Library*
& Museum 48

1

LONGFELLOW HOUSE & BRATTLE STREET

HIGHLIGHTS

- Longfellow's Study
- Chair made from the 'spreading chestnut tree'

DID YOU KNOW?

- Longfellow could speak 8 languages and read and write in 12

INFORMATION

- ✚ B2
- ✉ 105 Brattle Street, Cambridge
- ☎ 617/876 4492
- 🕐 Longfellow House closed until late 2000. Call to confirm opening
- 🍴 None
- Ⓣ Harvard (then pleasant ½ mile walk)
- ♿ Good
- 💲 Inexpensive
- ↔ Harvard Square and University (► 25), Harvard University Museums (► 26)
- ❓ House tours

The clapboard houses on Brattle Street in Cambridge are particularly beautiful examples of colonial architecture. One of them, Longfellow House, was Washington's base in the Revolution and later the home of one of America's best-loved poets.

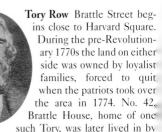

Tory Row Brattle Street begins close to Harvard Square. During the pre-Revolutionary 1770s the land on either side was owned by loyalist families, forced to quit when the patriots took over the area in 1774. No. 42, Brattle House, home of one such Tory, was later lived in by feminist author Margaret Fuller. The Dexter Pratt House, No. 56, now a bakery, was the home of the blacksmith of Longfellow's poem *The Village Blacksmith*. The shingle-fronted Stoughton House, No. 90, was designed by H H Richardson of Trinity Church fame (► 32).

Longfellow House No. 105, built in 1759 on an estate that extended down to the river, was George Washington's base during the siege of Boston, 1775–76. The widow of a later owner took in lodgers and thus, in 1837, came Henry Wadsworth Longfellow, the new Professor of Modern Languages at Harvard University. He later married Frances 'Fanny' Appleton, whose wealthy mill-owning father bought the house for them. Happily married, they raised six children here, entertaining the intellectuals of the day. It was here that Longfellow wrote many of his poems, including the *Song of Hiawatha* and *Paul Revere's Ride*. When renovation work is completed (late 2000), tour inside; until then, admire the fine yellow and white façade from the street.

Top: Longfellow House
Above: Henry Wadsworth Longfellow

HARVARD SQUARE & HARVARD UNIVERSITY

One of the most significant strands in the fabric of Bostonian life is the academic scene. In Cambridge you can walk through hallowed Harvard Yard in the footsteps of the great and famous, then enjoy the funky scene in Harvard Square.

Strolling through Harvard Square

Harvard University Among the first things the Massachusetts Bay colonists did was to provide for the training of ministers, and thus was founded, in 1636, what became one of the world's most respected seats of learning. Most of its historic buildings are in Harvard Yard, entered across the street from the First Parish Church. Ahead, in front of Bulfinch's granite University Hall, is a statue by Daniel Chester French of benefactor John Harvard, famous for its 'three lies' (Harvard was not the founder; a student, not Harvard, was the model; the foundation date is wrong). The elegant 18th-century redbrick halls grouped around this, the Old Yard, are dormitories. Behind University Hall is New Yard, with Memorial Church on the left facing the pillared façade of Widener Library. Groups of students move quietly across the grassy lawns. Pass beside H H Richardson's Sever Hall to emerge in Quincy Street opposite the Carpenter Center for the Visual Arts, the only Le Corbusier building in North America. The Fogg Art Museum (➤ 26) is next door. Radcliffe College, formerly a women's college, is alongside Cambridge Common, centred on the lovely Radcliffe Yard.

Harvard Square The newspaper stall by the T is a famous landmark in this irregularly shaped 'square'. In and around it you can watch chess games, listen to street musicians, sit outdoors in a café, shop for trendy clothes, browse in bookshops or go to a club for jazz, blues or reggae.

HIGHLIGHTS

- Harvard Yard
- Radcliffe Yard
- Browsing in a bookshop all evening

INFORMATION

- ✚ C2
- ✉ Harvard University: Harvard Yard, Peabody Street, Cambridge
- ☎ Visitor Information Booth 617/497 1630; University 617/495 1573
- 🕐 Daily
- 🍴 Plenty
- 🚇 Harvard
- 💲 Free
- ↔ Longfellow House (➤ 24), Harvard University Museums (➤ 26)
- ❓ Campus tours Mon–Fri 10, 2; Sat 2

3

HARVARD UNIVERSITY MUSEUMS

HIGHLIGHTS

- Italian early Renaissance paintings (Fogg)
- Impressionists (Fogg)
- Jade (Sackler)
- Glass flowers (Botanical)

INFORMATION

- ✚ C2
- ✉ Fogg & Busch-Reisinger: 32 Quincy Street. Sackler: 485 Broadway, Cambridge
  ☎ 617/495 9400 (both)
  Botanical: 24 Oxford Street; Peabody: 11 Divinity Avenue
  ☎ 617/495 3045
- 🕐 Mon–Sat 9–5 (Art Museums 10–5); Sun 1–5
- ♿ Very good
- 💲 Moderate. Art museums

*Top: Fogg Art Museum
Below: The Crucifixion by
Lorenzetti Ambrogio*

Few universities have such an enviable collection. The pieces in Harvard's three art museums, each of which has its own character, are of a quality to rival any in the world. Try to visit on a Wednesday or on Saturday morning – it's free then.

Fogg Art Museum The galleries of the Fogg Art Museum are arranged around a Renaissance-style arcaded courtyard, a delightful setting for a remarkable collection of Western art. The Italian early Renaissance period is particularly well represented, with gems from artists such as Simone Martini, Bernardo Daddi and Filippo Lippi. Other rooms cover Dutch and Flemish painting. Upstairs galleries feature major American landscape painters and an outstanding collection with familiar pieces by all the major Impressionists and some important Picassos.

Busch-Reisinger Museum Reached through the upper floor of the Fogg, this small museum focuses on Expressionist art of Central and Northern Europe, with Bauhaus artefacts and paintings by Kandinsky, Klee and Moholy-Nagy.

Arthur M Sackler Museum Next door to the Fogg, at the corner of Quincy Street and Broadway, the Sackler is in a building by Sir James Stirling. Along with one of the best collections of Chinese jade in the world, it has Chinese bronzes, Japanese prints, and Greek and Roman vases and sculptures – all superb examples.

Museums of Cultural & Natural History This is a large complex of four adjoining museums. For most visitors the highlight is the Botanical Museum's Glass Flowers exhibit, 3,000 glass models of 830 species of flower. The Peabody Museum is devoted to anthropology.

ISABELLA STEWART GARDNER MUSEUM

In this eclectically arranged art museum, one woman's personal collection of treasures displayed in the Venetian-style house she built around an exquisite courtyard, your mind is sure to get a mental workout.

'Beautiful things' Determined to give her 'very young country' the opportunity of 'seeing beautiful things', the much-travelled Mrs Gardner made a start in 1896 by buying a Rembrandt self-portrait. Her collection grew to include work by artists such as Giotto, Botticelli, Raphael, Vermeer, Degas and Matisse, as well as her friends John Singer Sargent and James McNeill Whistler. She also acquired prints and drawings, books, sculptures, ceramics and glass, carpets, tapestries, lace, stained glass, ironwork and furniture.

Music and horticulture The building itself, known as Fenway Court, and the atmosphere that pervades it, is as much the creation of Mrs Gardner as her collection. She arranged her objects in a series of rooms – the Raphael Room, the Titian Room, the Gothic Room, the intimate Blue Room (reopened in 1998 with its walls re-covered in newly woven silks replicating the originals) and more. She filled the courtyard with sculptures, plants and trees, and she celebrated the opening of her home (she lived on the top floor) to the public with a concert given by members of the Boston Symphony Orchestra. Today, concerts are held in the Tapestry Room on winter weekends.

Art heist The collection suffered a terrible loss – and America's biggest art theft – in March 1990 when thieves dressed as policemen made off with 13 items. Among them were a Vermeer and *The Sea of Galilee*, Rembrandt's only seascape. The pieces are still missing.

HIGHLIGHTS

- The courtyard, any season
- The restored Blue Room
- Afternoon concerts on winter weekends

INFORMATION

- ✚ D6
- ✉ 280 The Fenway, Back Bay
- ☎ 617/566 1401
- 🕐 Tue–Sun 11–5. Closed Mon except most public hols
- 🍴 On premises
- 🚇 Museum (green line E)
- ♿ Good
- 💲 Expensive. Boston CityPass applies
- ↔ Museum of Fine Arts (➤ 28)
- ❓ Concerts Sep–May: Sat, Sun 1:30 ☎ 617/734 1359. Tour Fri 2:30. Courtyard talks Tue–Fri 11:30, 1. Lectures, shop

The courtyard – fountains, ferns, and fragrant flowering plants

5

MUSEUM OF FINE ARTS

The MFA is one of America's foremost museums. The Asian collection is unrivalled in this hemisphere, the European art is superb, the American rooms excellent. If time is limited, focus your visit, or take a guided tour of the highlights.

HIGHLIGHTS

- Nubian collection
- Impressionist room
- Copley portraits
- Tang dynasty earthenware

INFORMATION

- ✚ E6
- ✉ 465 Huntington Avenue, Back Bay
- ☎ 617/267 9300
- 🕐 Mon, Tue 10–4:45; Wed–Fri 10–9:45 (Thu, Fri West Wing only after 5); Sat, Sun 10–5:45
- 🍴 Choice on premises
- Ⓜ Museum (green line E)
- ♿ Excellent
- 💲 Expensive. Wed 4–9:45 voluntary contribution. Boston CityPass applies
- ↔ Gardner Museum (► 27)
- ❓ Free guided walks Mon–Sat. Tea and Music Tue–Fri 2:30–4. Lectures, films, concerts. Good shop

Winslow Homer, Long Branch, *detail*

Asian, Egyptian, classical The MFA's Nubian collection is the best outside the Sudan. It is all exquisite, from the neat rows of little *shawabtis* (figurines) to the faience jewellery. The Egyptian rooms are popular, with mummies, hieroglyphics and splendid Old Kingdom sculptures. Buddhist sculptures, Chinese ceramics and Indian paintings make up part of an Asian collection outstanding in scope and quality. Outside, take in the Japanese Tenshin Garden (spring to autumn).

European In the Evans Wing upstairs, look out for the little gem of a Rembrandt in a glass case, then take in works of Tiepolo, Gainsborough, Turner, Delacroix, Constable and a good number of Millets. The Impressionist room is an array of familiar paintings, from Monet and Renoir to Gauguin. There is porcelain from all over Europe and period rooms from Britain.

American New England furniture and decorative arts feature in a series of period rooms. Near the silver (note Paul Revere's work) is a fine musical instruments collection. As for the art of New England, downstairs in the Evans Wing, begin with the Copley portraits, work through the 19th-century landscape painters Bierstadt, Fitz Hugh Lane and Thomas Cole, and move on to Winslow Homer and John Singer Sargent, and from the 20th century, Childe Hassam, Edward Hopper and Lilian Westacott Hale. In the Contemporary Art room find work by Georgia O'Keeffe and Stuart Davis.

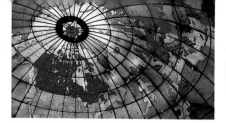

FIRST CHURCH OF CHRIST, SCIENTIST

The scale of this complex is mind-blowing. The world headquarters for the Church of Christ, Scientist, occupies 14 acres of prime Back Bay land, with a church seating 3,000. At its core is the truly remarkable Mapparium.

World headquarters Perhaps the best place from which to appreciate the vast size of the complex is from the top of the Prudential Tower (▶ 30). From here you look straight down on its 270-ft. reflecting pool with, alongside it, the small granite original Mother Church and the huge domed basilica-type extension. At the far end of the pool is the Publishing Society building, while nearer the Pru are the office tower, the Sunday School building and the Broadcasting Center.

The churches The Mother Church of Christian Science was founded in Boston in 1892 by Mary Baker Eddy. The original church building was opened in 1894 but the numbers of believers in spiritual healing grew so rapidly that an extension was built in 1906, seating 3,000. The huge open space here is dominated by one of the world's largest organs, played at every service.

Publishing and the Mapparium The *Christian Science Monitor* is a highly respected international daily newspaper, founded in 1908 by Mary Baker Eddy and read by many outside the movement for its unbiased reporting. The Publishing Society building also houses the Mapparium, a huge brightly coloured stained-glass globe. You can walk inside it and stand at the centre of the world. It shows the political boundaries of the early 1930s, when it was made. Try out the echo – sound waves bounce back off the glass, creating decidedly weird effects.

Top: Mapparium
Above: the Mother Church

DID YOU KNOW?

- The Mapparium has 608 panels, each covering 10 degrees of latitude and longitude
- The Aeolian-Skinner church organ has 13,595 pipes

INFORMATION

- ✚ F6
- ✉ 175 Huntington Avenue
- ☎ 617/450 2000
- ⏰ Mapparium closed until 2000; phone for opening times. Mother Church phone for times
- 🍴 Nearby in Prudential Center
- 🚇 Prudential
- ♿ Good
- 🎟 Free
- ↔ Prudential Tower Skywalk (▶ 30)
- ❓ Tours of the Mother Church

29

7

PRUDENTIAL & HANCOCK TOWERS

HIGHLIGHTS

- Reflection of Trinity Church
- Walter Muir Whitehill's voice-over (Hancock)
- Model of Boston in 1775 (Hancock)

INFORMATION

John Hancock Observatory

- ✚ F5
- ✉ Copley Square
- ☎ 617/572 6429
- 🕐 Mon–Sun 9AM–11PM (Sun 6PM Nov–Mar). Last ticket sold 1 hour before closing. Closed in bad weather
- 🍴 Nearby
- Ⓟ Copley
- ♿ Excellent
- 🎫 Inexpensive. Boston CityPass applies
- ↔ Boston Public Library (► 31), Trinity Church (► 32)

Prudential Skywalk

- ✚ F6
- ✉ Prudential Tower, 800 Boylston Street
- ☎ 617/859 0648
- 🕐 Daily 10–10. Closed in bad weather
- 🍴 Top of the Hub
- Ⓟ Prudential
- ♿ Excellent
- 🎫 Inexpensive
- ↔ First Church of Christ, Scientist (► 29)

The Hancock Tower seen
from the Pru

The bird's eye view of Boston, the harbour and its islands, the Charles River, Cambridge and the surrounding New England countryside is mezmerising from both these skyscrapers. Try to do one in the daytime and the other after dark.

John Hancock Tower & Observatory There is something immensely serene about this icy shaft of blue glass thrusting upward to join the clouds, no matter how ephemeral it looks beside Trinity Church, whose solid granite is reflected in its lowest windows. Designed by Henry Cobb of I M Pei & Partners in 1976 for the John Hancock Insurance Company, the building caused a mighty sensation at first, particularly when its panes of glass kept popping out and smashing on the sidewalk below. But it has long since found a place in (most) Bostonians' hearts. An express lift whisks you to the Observatory on the 60th floor; windows on three sides give all-round views. A delightful voice-over account by the architectural historian Walter Muir Whitehill of the city's changing topography guides you round the view and a sound-and-light show features the events of 1775. You can also tune in to Logan air traffic controllers' radios.

Skywalk at the Prudential Tower Architecturally undistinguished, the Prudential Tower is part of the 1960s Prudential Center office and shopping complex. Take the wind-whistling elevator to the Skywalk View and Exhibit on the 50th floor for 360-degree views as far as (weather permitting) the hills of Vermont. Various interactive exhibits fill you in on some of Boston's great historical and sports events, as well as its most distinguished buildings and residents. On the 52nd floor is Top of the Hub bar and restaurant.

BOSTON PUBLIC LIBRARY

This is no ordinary public library. Behind its august granite façade lies an opulent institution built in the style of a Renaissance palazzo and decorated with sculptures, murals and paintings by some of the greatest artists of their day.

The education of the people A people's palace dedicated to the advancement of learning was what Charles Follen McKim was commissioned to design. An architectural landmark in the classical style, facing Richardson's Romanesque Trinity Church across Copley Square, it opened its doors to the public in 1895. It is now the Research Library, the General Library being housed in the adjoining 1972 Johnson Building.

Further treasures Pass between Bela Pratt's voluptuous bronzes, *Science* and *Art*, to enter through Daniel Chester French's bronze doors. Pause in the lobby to admire the zodiac patterning of the marble floor and the mosaic ceiling. Ascend the marble staircase, guarded by lions by Louis Saint-Gaudens (Augustus's brother), and from its windows catch a glimpse of the peaceful courtyard around which the library is built. The stairs and landing are decorated with panels by Puvis de Chavannes, whimsical representations of the muses of inspiration. One room on this floor has paintings depicting the quest for the Holy Grail, by Edwin Austin Abbey. On the next floor are the John Singer Sargent murals, *Judaism* and *Christianity*, completed in 1916 and now awaiting restoration. Back downstairs, pass the silent reading rooms to find the colonnaded courtyard. Purple-leaved maples shade a pool bordered by dark green foliage. Sit for a while and enjoy the tranquillity.

HIGHLIGHTS

- The courtyard
- Puvis de Chavannes murals
- John Singer Sargent murals
- Daniel Chester French bronze doors

INFORMATION

- ✚ F5
- ✉ Copley Square
- ☎ 617/536 5400
- 🕐 Mon–Thu 9–9; Fri, Sat 9–5. Oct–May: Sun 1–5. Jun–Sep: closed Sun
- 🍴 Nearby
- Ⓜ Copley
- ♿ Good
- 💲 Free
- ↔ John Hancock Tower (➤ 30), Trinity Church (➤ 32)
- ❓ Art and architecture tours (Dartmouth Street entrance) Mon 2:30; Tue, Thu 6; Fri, Sat 11. Oct–May: Sun 2. Lectures

Top: staircase
Below: courtyard

9

TRINITY CHURCH

Top: La Farge murals
Above: west front

HIGHLIGHTS

- Polychrome interior
- John La Farge paintings and lancet windows
- Reflection in John Hancock Tower
- Christmas candlelight services

INFORMATION

- ✚ F5
- ✉ Copley Square
- ☎ 617/536 0944
- 🕐 Daily 8–6
- 🍴 Nearby
- Ⓠ Copley
- ♿ Good
- 🎟 Free
- ↔ John Hancock Tower (► 30), Boston Public Library (► 31)
- ❓ Free half-hour organ recitals Fri 12:15. Sun services 8, 9, 11 (with choir music), 6

H H Richardson's prototype French Romanesque church is often described as America's masterpiece of ecclesiastical architecture. Sit beneath its mighty tower: a greater contrast to the fragility of John Hancock Tower next door can hardly be imagined.

The plan The Back Bay was a newly developed landfill area when the Copley Square site was bought and Henry Hobson Richardson was commissioned, in 1872, to draw up designs for a new Trinity Church. Richardson based his layout on 11th-century Romanesque churches in the Auvergne, in France. A massive lantern tower over the transept crossing would dominate the church inside and out, requiring over 2,000 wooden piles massed together to support its granite foundations. Externally, the chunky granite blocks are broken up by bands of pink sandstone.

The interior Inside, John La Farge created an intricate polychrome interior, a tapestry of rich reds and greens highlighted with gold. The arches beneath the great tower are decorated with La Farge murals painted in 1876–7, and it was he who supervised the stained glass, some by Edward Burne-Jones and William Morris. La Farge's own small but vibrant, turquoise lancet windows are in the north transept, west wall. The decorated pipes of the organ in the west end are notable (music at Trinity is important). In the Baptistry is a bust by Daniel Chester French of the portly rector Phillips Brooks, whose greatest claim to fame is his carol 'O Little Town of Bethlehem'. His full-length statue, by Augustus Saint-Gaudens, stands outside the north transept. At the east end there is a small cloister and garden.

BACK BAY & COMMONWEALTH AVENUE

A Parisian-style boulevard lined with the grandest houses in Boston is the centre-piece of an amazing piece of 19th-century urban planning. To walk down it is to be transported to a different age.

Landfill By the 1850s, Boston, still a small peninsula, was getting overcrowded. Desperate for building land, developers turned to the swampy 'back bay' of the Charles River, embarking on a remarkable landfill project to create a whole new residential district. Inspired by Paris's boulevard system, the architect Arthur Gilman planned a grid, eight blocks long and four blocks wide, with a long central mall. Block by block, the new houses went up and the wealthy moved in.

Commonwealth Avenue The nouveau-riche industrialists who flocked to the Back Bay felt none of the Puritan restraints of the Proper Bostonians of Beacon Hill, and their rows of ostentatious brownstones are an exuberant blend of Victorian architectural styles. The centrepiece is Commonwealth Avenue. Central gardens are lined with trees; in spring magnolias bloom in profusion. A string of statues includes slavery abolitionist William Lloyd Garrison and naval historian Samuel Eliot Morison. Find your own favourite houses – almost every one has something worthy of note. Most are now apartments, some are offices. The château-like Burrage Mansion at Hereford Street stands out, with statuettes all over the place. To see inside a more average home, visit Gibson House on Beacon Street (► 52). After strolling down Commonwealth Avenue, walk back along Newbury Street for some stylish window-shopping (► 70). Also check out the Newbury Street *trompe l'oeil* murals at the Boston Architectural Center and No. 354.

Samuel Eliot Morison statue, Commonwealth Avenue

HIGHLIGHTS

- Houses on Commonwealth Avenue
- Window-shopping in Newbury Street
- People-watching in the Newbury Street cafés

DID YOU KNOW?

- North–south streets are named alphabetically, Arlington to Hereford

INFORMATION

- F5–G5
- Newbury and Boylston Streets
- Arlington, Copley, Hynes
- First Church of Christ, Scientist (► 29), Hancock Tower (► 30), Prudential Tower (► 30), Boston Public Library (► 31), Trinity Church (► 32), Public Garden (► 36)

11

MUSEUM OF SCIENCE

This whole place buzzes and hums with excited children running around pressing buttons and peering into things. The 600 interactive (and frequently changing) exhibits make for a stimulating visit.

HIGHLIGHTS

- Lightning demo
- Best Software for Kids gallery
- Virtual FishTank
- Exercising your skeleton
- Mugar Omni Theater shows

INFORMATION

- ✚ G3
- ✉ Science Park
- ☎ 617/723 2500
- ⊙ 5 Jul–Labor Day: daily 9–7 (Fri 9–9). Labor Day–4 Jul: daily 9–5 (Fri 9–9). Extended hours over school hols
- 🍴 Three on premises
- Ⓠ Science Park
- ♿ Excellent. Sight and hearing impaired facilities
- 🎟 Expensive. Separate tickets for Planetarium, Laser Show, Omni Theater. Combination ticket discounts. Boston CityPass applies
- ❓ Good shop

Science now In 1999 the Science Museum took on board the former Computer Museum, a move that underlines how computer technologies have revolutionised science. The complex straddles the Charles River, with fine views of the Cambridge and Boston skylines.

'It's awesome' Start with the dramatic indoor lightning demos in the Theater of Electricity, where the world's largest Van de Graaff generator creates 2.5 million volts of electricity. Here too is the popular Best Software for Kids gallery. A 20-ft T Rex peers over the rails from the Lower Level, and in the Virtual FishTank, near the Wave Tank, you can create a fish, programme its behaviour and see what happens when you release it into the ocean. Other popular exhibits include the Human Body Connection, with its exercising skeleton, and the Live Animal Stage, where you come face to face with snakes, owls and porcupines. Seeing is Deceiving explores illusions, visual and auditory, while in the Science in the Park you can and find out why a swing swings.

Mugar Omni, Planetarium and Lasers Lie back and be totally enveloped in the sight and sound of an IMAX film in the five-storey domed screen of the Mugar Omni Theater with its digital sound system. Multi-media presentations at the Planetarium cover various astronomical subjects, and there are evening laser programmes.

BEACON HILL & LOUISBURG SQUARE

Beacon Hill is an enclave of elegant redbrick houses in a leafy maze of steep streets and narrow cobbled lanes and is a delightful area to explore. It has been the bastion of the Boston Brahmin since the early 1800s.

Brahmin stronghold After the opening of the new State House on its southern slope, Beacon Hill was developed as a prestigious residential district by a group of entrepreneurs that included architect Charles Bulfinch (► 12). Boston's top families swiftly moved in. Rich as they were, these Brahmins were also the personification of Puritan reserve. Showiness was taboo, so their new houses were the epitome of restraint, with elegant doorways and delicate ironwork gracing plain brick façades.

Perfectly preserved To get the magic of it all, choose a sunny day and just wander, noting the pillared porticoes, genteel fanlights, and flowery window boxes. The Beacon Hill walk (► 16) leads you to some of the most treasured corners, including Mt Vernon Street, Chestnut Street, tiny Acorn Street and, best of all, Louisburg Square. Here Bulfinch's lovely bowfronts look onto a central garden reminiscent of a European square. Notice how the street lamps are lit all day and, in Beacon Street, look for the purple panes: manganese oxide in a batch of glass reacted with sunlight to produce discoloured but, now, highly prized and very distinctive panes. To see inside a Beacon Hill home, visit the Nichols House (► 53). On the hill's north slope from Pinckney Street down to Cambridge Street, the houses are smaller and more varied in style, the overall effect less grand. It has several important sites in the history of Boston's African-American community (► 53).

HIGHLIGHTS

- Louisburg Square
- Pinckney Street and its view of Charles River
- Purple panes of glass, Beacon Street
- Charles Street shops and restaurants

INFORMATION

- ✚ a–b III–IV; G4
- ✉ Bounded by Beacon Street, Embankment Road, Cambridge Street, Bowdoin Street
- 🍴 Choice in Charles Street
- Ⓜ Park, Charles, Arlington, Bowdoin (closed Sat)
- ♿ Steep hills, some uneven surfaces
- ↔ Boston Common & Public Garden (► 36), Harrison Gray Otis House (► 37), State House (► 38), Beacon Street & Boston Athenaeum (► 39)
- ❓ SPNEA tours of Beacon Hill (► 37), Black Heritage Trail: see Museum of Afro-American History (► 53)

BOSTON COMMON & THE PUBLIC GARDEN

Top: Swan Boats, Public Garden
Above: Boston Common

DID YOU KNOW?

● The Swan Boats were inspired by Wagner's *Lohengrin*

INFORMATION

✚ aIV–bIV; G5

✉ Bounded by Beacon, Park, Tremont, Boylston, Arlington streets

☎ Swan Boats 617/522 1966. Ice-skating 617/635 2120

⏰ Public Garden daily dawn–10PM. Swan Boats Apr–Sep. Ice-skating Nov–Mar

🍴 Nearby

Ⓟ Park, Boylston, Arlington

✋ Garden and Common free. Swan Boats, skating cheap

↔ Beacon Hill (▶ 35), Harrison Gray Otis House (▶ 37), State House (▶ 38), Beacon Street & Boston Athenaeum (▶ 39)

Very different in history and in character, these adjoining pieces of public open space, separated by Charles Street, right in the heart of the city, are held in deep affection. Without them, Boston just wouldn't be Boston.

Boston Common The oldest public park in the United States owes its origins to early British settlers who in 1634 acquired the land from a Reverend William Blaxton for common grazing. Being common land, it was also where criminals were hanged, witches were dunked and the dead were buried (in the Central Burying Ground, by Boylston Street). Here, British soldiers camped and George Washington addressed the crowds after Independence. Early in the 1800s the gallows were removed, cattle were banned, paths were laid out, fountains and monuments erected. It is still a place for speeches and demos, but also for sports, for paddling or, in winter, ice-skating on Frog Pond, chasing the pigeons, eating ice cream, listening to street performers and concerts – and people-watching. Perfectly safe by day, it's best avoided at night.

The Public Garden Much more genteel and decorative, this was created as a botanical garden in 1837 from reclaimed marshland. Hundreds of beautiful trees were planted, and beds, lawns and a lacing of footpaths were laid out. The garden is perennially beautiful and often fairytale-like. The centrepiece is a pond, with a little cast-iron suspension bridge. Here, in summer, you can ride the famous Swan Boats and, in winter, you can skate. Sculptures include an equestrian *George Washington* (Thomas Ball, 1869), Bela Pratt's *Edward Everett Hale* (1913), the Ether Monument, marking its first use as an anaesthetic in 1846 and *Make Way for Ducklings* (▶ 59).

HARRISON GRAY OTIS HOUSE

This is Boston's only remaining example of a Federal-style mansion. Meticulously restored in its every detail, the gracious interior is a very accurate representation of how the upper classes lived in the 19th century.

Otis and Bulfinch One of the leading lights in post-Revolutionary Boston politics was the lawyer Harrison Gray Otis (1765–1844), long-standing friend of architect Charles Bulfinch. A wealthy man moving in the upper echelons of Bostonian society, in 1796 he commissioned Bulfinch to build him this grand mansion in what was then the elegant area of Bowdoin Square. The structure's very restrained, very proper, brick façade is typical of what became known as the Federal style. Five years later, Bulfinch built Otis an even bigger house on newly developed Beacon Hill (➤ 35), to which all the wealthy were rapidly migrating. By the 1830s the Otis home had become a boarding house. Now the Otis House and the Old West Church next door are a little oasis of elegance in an area of less-than-lovely urban renewal.

The SPNEA In 1916 the Society for the Preservation of New England Antiquities bought the property as its headquarters. Accuracy and authenticity being its hallmarks, the SPNEA has restored the interior with reproduction wall-papers and paint colours based on paint analysis (there are some surprisingly bright yellows and turquoises). Otis and his wife, Sally, were lavish entertainers and the parlour, dining room and first-floor drawing room, all brightly coloured and furnished in high Federal style, provide an insight into social manners of the day, while bedrooms, kitchens and servant quarters give you a glimpse of family life.

HIGHLIGHTS

- Bulfinch Federal design
- Reproductions of original wallpaper
- Colours of original paintwork
- Federal era furniture

DID YOU KNOW?

- In 1926 the house was moved back 40 feet because of road widening

INFORMATION

- ✚ bIII; G4
- ✉ 141 Cambridge Street
- ☎ 617/227 3956
- 🕐 Wed–Sun 11–5. Tours on the hour. Last tour at 4
- 🍴 None
- Ⓜ Bowdoin (closed Sat), Charles, Government Center
- ♿ Wheelchairs ground floor only
- ✋ Moderate. SPNEA members free
- ↔ Beacon Hill (➤ 35), State House (➤ 38), Boston Athenaeum (➤ 39)
- ❓ Walking tours of Beacon Hill mid-May to mid-Oct, Sat (call ahead). Shop

15

MASSACHUSETTS STATE HOUSE

HIGHLIGHTS

- Gold dome (reguilded 1998 with 22 carat gold leaf)
- Sacred Cod
- Senate Reception Room
- Senate Chamber

DID YOU KNOW?

- When the Sacred Cod was stolen by students in 1933, no sessions could be held for three days
- If Republicans gain power, the Sacred Cod will be turned to face the other way
- From 1825 to 1928 the brick facade was painted
- Road distances out of Boston are measured from the dome

INFORMATION

- ✛ bIII–bIV; G4
- ✉ Beacon Street
- ☎ 617/727 3676
- ◷ Mon–Sat 10–4
- 🍴 None
- 🚇 Park
- ♿ Partial wheelchair access
- 👆 Free
- ↔ Beacon Hill (➤ 35), Harrison Gray Otis House (➤ 37), Boston Athenaeum (➤ 39)
- ❓ Regular tours (45 minutes)

Prosperous and newly independent in the late 18th century, Massachusetts needed a larger, more imposing State House. Charles Bulfinch's masterpiece is a landmark in American architecture.

Hub of the Hub Bulfinch began designing the new state house on his return from England, much influenced by Robert Adam's Renaissance style. Construction began in 1795 on a prominent piece of Beacon Hill land presented by the wealthy merchant and patriot John Hancock. Cut off in your mind's eye the side wings (an early 20th-century addition), and focus on Bulfinch's dignified two-storey portico and the glistening dome. Its original shingles were covered in copper from the foundry of Paul Revere when the roof began to leak, and the gold leaf was added in 1874.

Seat of government At the top of the steps, go through a side door into the columned Doric Hall (the central door is for visiting presidents and retiring governors only). From here pass through the marble Nurses' Hall and note Bela Pratt's memorial to Civil War nurses. The Italian marble floor in the Hall of Flags was laid by immigrants from Italy living in the North End. Featured in the stained-glass skylight are the seats of the original 13 states. Up the staircase is the House of Representatives chamber. Here, the Sacred Cod, a symbol of the importance of the fishing industry and a lucky mascot, must hang whenever the 160 state representatives are in session. The dignified barrel-vaulted and Ionic-columned Senate Reception Room is Bulfinch's, as is the Senate Chamber, where 40 senators debate beneath a graceful sunburst dome. A larger-than-life *JFK* (Isabel McIlvain, 1988) is one of several statues outside.

BEACON STREET & THE ATHENAEUM

Beacon Street flaunts one or two well-known landmarks – the State House and, indeed, Cheers! – but this elegant street also holds gems of a more discreet nature.

'Haunt of all the most civilised' 10½ Beacon Street (to your right as you face the State House) is home to the Boston Athenaeum, founded in 1807 to foster scholarship, literature, science and the visual arts. By the time it moved here, it had been the centre of intellectual and cultural life for over 40 years. Indeed, the paintings and sculptures it had accumulated were to form the core of the Museum of Fine Arts' founding collections. It remains an oasis of civility, a library where members leave the hassle of daily life behind to peruse a periodical in a leather armchair, browse in the open stacks or take tea in a reading room laden with oriental rugs, paintings, sculptures and flowers. Visitors, however, must wait till 2001 to take a tour, as the building is being restored – it's well worth the wait.

Highlights Facing the State House (➤ 38) is the monument (➤ 55) to young Robert Gould Shaw leading his black regiment down Beacon Street past his home, No. 44, to death in the Civil War, as depicted in the film *Glory*. Down hill are mirror-image Nos. 39 and 40; at 39 Fanny Appleton married the poet Longfellow in 1843. Watch for Beacon Street's famous purple panes of glass (➤ 37). No. 45 was the third house built by Charles Bulfinch for Harrison Gray Otis (➤ 37). Historian William Prescott lived at 55, composing entirely in his head. And you can't miss 84: the setting for the TV show *Cheers!* was the Bull and Finch pub, shipped in from England. Beyond Arlington Street, the Gibson House Museum (➤ 52) is flanked by Emerson and Fisher colleges.

HIGHLIGHTS

- Tours of the Boston Athenaeum (from 2001)
- Robert Gould Shaw monument
- Massachusetts State House
- Views over the Boston Common
- Purple panes

INFORMATION

- ✚ cIV; G4–G5
- ⊙ The Boston Athenaeum
  - ✉ 10½ Beacon Street; closed till 2001
  - ☎ 617/227 0270
  - Massachusetts State House (➤ 38)
  - Gibson House Museum (➤ 52)
- 🍴 Park Street, Beacon Street and Charles Street
- Ⓟ Park Street
- ↔ Beacon Hill and Louisburg Square (➤ 35), Boston Common & the Public Garden (➤ 36), Harrison Gray Otis House (➤ 37)

OLD SOUTH MEETING HOUSE

HIGHLIGHTS

- Plain Puritan interior
- Box pews
- Tea Party audios

INFORMATION

- dIV; H5
- Washington Street at Milk Street
- 617/482 6439
- Apr–Oct: daily 9:30–5. Nov–Mar: daily 10–5
- Nearby
- State, Downtown Crossing
- Good
- Inexpensive
- Old State House (➤ 41)
- Concerts, lectures, tours. Shop

Portrait of early settler etched onto glass

What started life in 1729 as a traditional Puritan meeting house was later, by reason only of its size, to witness one of the most significant moments in American and British history.

Sanctuary of freedom When things started to heat up in the years leading up to the Revolution, the town hall, Faneuil Hall, could no longer hold the crowds that were turning up, so this, the most spacious meeting place in the city, became their venue. Here the sparks of insurrection fanned by such speakers as Samuel Adams, James Otis and John Hancock ignited on the evening of 16 December 1773. For it was here that night that Adams famously declared 'Gentlemen, this meeting can do nothing more to save the country' – the signal for a band of men disguised as Mohawk Indians to lead the people off to the harbour and the so-called Boston Tea Party (➤ 12).

A chequered history In the siege of Boston that followed, British troops occupied Old South, ripping out the pews and using it as a riding school for the cavalry. After the Revolution, it was restored as a church, but in 1872 was replaced by the New Old South Church, located on the corner of Copley Square. Threatened with demolition, Old South was saved for its historical associations and has been a museum ever since. The plain white-painted pews and pulpit of this simple brick church are reproductions, but the two-tiered gallery is original. Visual displays tell the story of Old South and audios of fiery debates describe the whole Tea Party event in graphic detail.

OLD STATE HOUSE

This is the city's oldest public building, once the seat of British colonial government. Surrounded by taller – but far less significant – buildings, it seems so tiny now. It holds a first-rate museum.

Colonial capitol Built in 1713 to replace an earlier Town House, the Old State House was the British governor's seat of office, home to the judicial court and to the Massachusetts Assembly. As such it was the scene of many a confrontation between the colonists and their rulers. It was here that James Otis railed against the 'tyranny of taxation without representation' and it was under the balcony at the east end that the 'Boston Massacre' took place in 1770: five colonists were killed in a clash with British soldiers, a key event in the years leading up to the Revolution. From the same balcony, the Declaration of Independence was read on 18 July 1776. At this point the gilded lion and unicorn on the east front, symbols of the British Crown, were destroyed. From 1780 until Bulfinch's new State House was opened on Beacon Hill in 1798, this was the Massachusetts State House. For most of the 19th century it was used for commercial purposes, gradually falling into disrepair until the Boston Society was founded in 1881 to restore the building. The lion and unicorn were returned to their place, balanced now by the American eagle and the Massachusetts seal on the west end.

A museum of Boston The building is now home to the Bostonian Society's excellent museum. It traces the city's topographical, political, economic and social history with a fine collection of maritime art and artefacts, revolutionary memorabilia, prints, domestic objects and audio exhibits.

HIGHLIGHTS

- Lion and unicorn
- Balcony from which Declaration of Independence was read
- Exhibit showing typographical changes
- Vial of tea from the Tea Party

INFORMATION

- ✛ clll; H4
- ✉ 206 Washington Street
- ☎ 617/720 3290
- 🕓 Daily 9–5
- 🍴 Nearby
- 🚇 State
- ♿ No access to upper floor
- 💰 Inexpensive
- ↔ Old South Meeting House (➤ 40), Faneuil Hall (➤ 42)
- ❓ Shop

19

FANEUIL HALL & MARKETPLACE

Faneuil Hall

HIGHLIGHTS

- Bulfinch meeting room
- Grasshopper weathervane on the roof
- Quincy's granite market buildings
- Street entertainers
- Food hall

INFORMATION

- ✚ dlll; H4
- ✉ Congress Street
- ☎ 617/242 5642
- 🕐 Faneuil Hall meeting room 9–5 (when not in use)
- 🍴 A plethora
- Ⓜ State, Aquarium, Government Center
- ♿ Good
- 🎫 Meeting room free
- ↔ Old State House (➤ 41)
- ❓ Meeting room: 15-minute talk every ½ hour

Faneuil Hall is a landmark for all Americans, the place where the iniquities of the British government were first debated in the 1770s. Nowadays its marketplace is a landmark for visitors of every nation – as well as for Bostonians.

The Cradle of Liberty A wealthy trader of Huguenot origins, Peter Faneuil (pronounced either 'Fannel' or to rhyme with Daniel), presented the town with a market hall with a meeting room above. Ever since, the lower hall has been a market, and the galleried upper hall has been a place for public gatherings. In the 1700s, because the town meetings frequently discussed the problems with Britain that lead up to the revolution and independence, Faneuil Hall became known as America's Cradle of Liberty. Since then national issues from the abolition of slavery to the Vietnam War have been aired here. If it is not in use, it's worth going in to hear the guide's account of the Revolution. The room bears all the trademarks of Bulfinch, who expanded it in 1805.

Quincy's marketplace The Bulfinch expansion soon proved to be inadequate as more space was needed. In 1826, with an inspired piece of town planning that radically changed Boston's waterfront, mayor Josiah Quincy filled in Town Dock and built over the wharves, providing a granite market hall flanked by granite warehouses. These were a wholesale food market until the 1960s. In the 1970s the area was renovated and revitalised, and is now the city's main tourist attraction (known as either Faneuil Hall Marketplace or Quincy Market) with dozens of shops, barrows, stalls, eating places and street entertainers. The Durgin Park Dining Rooms are an institution (➤ 62).

USS *Constitution* & Charlestown

'Old Ironsides', as she is widely known by schoolchildren, is the oldest commissioned warship afloat in the world. Over 200 year old, she is moored in the Charlestown Navy Yard, a short, pleasant boat ride away across the Charles River.

The Navy Yard From 1800 to 1974 the Charles River navy yard played an important role building, repairing and supplying Navy warships. Its mission now is to interpret the history of naval shipbuilding. Representing the ships built here are USS *Constitution* and the World War II destroyer USS *Cassin Young*, both of which may be boarded. The old granite Building 22 now houses the USS *Constitution* Museum, where journals, artefacts and other exhibits record the frigate's 200-year career in both war and peace and give a picture of life aboard. Also open is the Commandant's House. The Bunker Hill Pavilion's multimedia show, 'Whites of Their Eyes', tells the story of the Battle of Bunker Hill, which actually took place nearby on Breed's Hill, on which stands the Bunker Hill Monument (► 55). The Monument is visible from and within walking distance of the yard.

USS *Constitution* The highlight of the Navy Yard is 'Old Ironsides'. Launched in Boston in 1797, she is still part of the US Navy, whose sailors lead tours round the cramped quarters and stand proudly by the neat coils of black and white rope, glistening brass and rows of guns. Vulnerable though the wooden sides seem now, it was her tough live-oak frames that enabled her to survive the War of 1812 undefeated and win her her nickname. A frail old lady, heavily reconstructed, she takes a turn in the harbour every year on 4 July, changing the side that faces the elements.

HIGHLIGHTS

- Museum: details of sailor's daily diet and duties
- USS *Constitution*: cramped lower deck

INFORMATION

- ✚ H3
- ✉ Charlestown Navy Yard
- ☎ Navy Yard visitor centre 617/242 5601. 'Whites of Their Eyes' reservations 617/241 7575
- ◷ USS *Constitution* main deck 9:30–15 minutes before dusk; lower deck by guided tour only 9:30–3:50. USS *Cassin Young* main deck 10–5 (4 in winter); lower deck by guided tour only 10–4 (3 in winter). Museum May–Oct: daily 9–6. Nov–Apr: daily 10–5. Bunker Hill Pavilion 'White of Their Eyes' Apr–1 Dec: daily 9:30–4
- ♯ In the yard
- Ⓢ North station, then 10–15-minute walk
- ⛴ MBTA Water Shuttle from Long Wharf
- ♿ All wheelchair accessible except USS *Cassin Young*
- Ⓜ All free except 'Whites of Their Eyes' inexpensive
- ❓ Summer tours Navy Yard (11AM). Museum shop

43

THE NORTH END & OLD NORTH CHURCH

HIGHLIGHTS

- Paul Revere House
  (➤ 45)
- Old North Church
- Copp's Hill Burying Ground
  (➤ 56)
- Feast day processions
- Italian groceries

INFORMATION

- ✛ d–c l–ll; H3–H4
- ✉ Bounded by Commercial Street and (roughly) the expressway
- 🍴 Plenty in and around Hanover and Salem Streets
- Ⓜ Haymarket, North station, Aquarium, State
- ♿ Some hills
- ↔ Paul Revere House
  (➤ 45)
- ❓ Tour Old North Church, climb the steeple
  Ⓖ Jun–Oct

The North End is Boston's oldest and most spirited district. This is where the British colonists settled in the 1600s, and now, after various ups and downs, it is a lively Italian quarter.

Little Italy The North End is separated from the rest of Boston by the JFK Expressway, also known as the Central Artery (while work on putting it below ground continues, take the walkway underneath). When the colonists arrived it was also all but cut off, surrounded then by water at the end of a narrow peninsula. The colonists' erratic street plan survives, but the only building from the 17th century is Paul Revere House (➤ 45). Once the elite had moved to Beacon Hill in the early 1800s, the area played host to waves of immigrants, first the Irish, then East European and Portuguese and finally Italians. It is the Italians who have given the area its current flavour, with Italian spoken in the streets, Italian pop music playing in the cafés and lively weekend street festivals in July and August.

Old North Church St Stephen's Church (➤ 56) in the main artery of Hanover Street faces Revere's statue (➤ 55) and, behind it, the tall white steeple of Old North Church. It was from Old North that Revere's signal was given to the patriots in Charlestown that the British were on their way to Lexington where, the next day, the first battle of the War of Independence took place. Up the hill from Old North is the Copp's Hill Burying Ground (➤ 56). From here wind down Snowhill and through the tall narrow streets to Salem Street and, perhaps, a treat from a *pasticceria*.

Old North steeple

PAUL REVERE HOUSE

This rare example of early colonial archi-tecture is all that remains of the 17th-century settlement in today's North End. Not only is it Boston's oldest building, it was also the home of its most celebrated son, Paul Revere.

The early years The steep-gabled clapboard house that we see today was built in about 1680. Like most houses of the period, it had two rooms on each of its two floors but the position-ing of the main staircase at the side of the building, making the rooms larger than normal, was unusual. By 1770, when the silversmith and engraver Paul Revere (► 12) came to live here, a number of significant alterations had been made, notably the addition of a third floor and a two-storey extension at the back. The family lived here during the Revolution, so it was from here that Revere set out on that famous midnight ride. In 1800, after the family sold the house, it became a rooming house, with shops and factory premises on the lower floor. Threatened with demolition in 1902, it was saved by Revere's great-grand-son and, restored to something like its origins, became a museum.

The house today The basic timber skeleton of the house is the original, but the exterior clapboarding, the windows and most of what you see inside are replacements. Go through the kitchen into the living room, furnished in period style. Upstairs, the main bedroom is an elegantly furnished room, which would have doubled as a parlour. In the other room, note the ingenious folding bed and its traditional woven cover.

HIGHLIGHTS

- Revere's own account of his ride
- Period furnishings

INFORMATION

- ✚ dII; H4
- ✉ 19 North Square
- ☎ 617/523 2338
- 🕐 Nov—mid-Apr: daily 9:30—4:15. Mid-Apr—Oct: daily 9:30—5:15. Jan—Mar: closed Mon
- 🍴 Nearby
- Ⓜ Government Center, State, Aquarium, Haymarket
- ♿ Wheelchair access lower floor only
- 💵 Inexpensive
- ↔ Old North Church (► 44)
- ❓ Tours of early Georgian Pierce/Hichborn House

Bronze bell cast by Paul Revere

NEW ENGLAND AQUARIUM

HIGHLIGHTS

- Giant Ocean Tank
- Watching tank divers
- The huge green sea turtle
- Little Blue penguins
- 'Sounds of the Sea' exhibit
- Whalewatch trip
- 'Science at Sea' harbour trip

INFORMATION

- dlll; J4
- Central Wharf
- 617/973 5200
- 1 Jul–Labor Day: Mon, Tue, Fri 9–6; Wed, Thu 9–8; Sat, Sun, hols 9–7. Rest of year: Mon–Fri 9–5; Sat, Sun, hols 9–6
- On premises
- Aquarium
- Good
- Expensive. Boston CityPass applies
- Whalewatch trips Apr–Oct 617/973–5281. Harbour tours Jul, Aug. Shop

Housing one of the largest aquatic collections in the world, this is a popular family excursion. A spiral ramp leads you around a vast cyclindrical tank that swirls with myriad sea creatures of every imaginable size, shape and colour.

Exhibits Take in the outdoor seal exhibit before you enter. Once inside, head left and in the penguin pool at the base of the Giant Ocean Tank pick out the world's smallest species, the Little Blues. Either go outside to catch a sea lion presentation or turn right, up the straight ramp, to the Thinking Gallery, where you can compare your hearing to that of a dolphin and your skeleton to that of a fish. The Freshwater Gallery has above- and below-surface views of a flooded Amazon forest complete with anaconda, alongside, by contrast, a New England trout stream. Don't miss the electric eel. Eventually, you reach the top of the huge tank at the centre of the Aquarium. At feeding times, approximately hourly, staff dive in, scattering squid for the bigger fish, jamming lettuce into the fibreglass coral reef for the angel fish, hand-feeding the sharks and giving the turtles their vitamin-enriched gelatin (to keep their shells hard). Notice how all the fish swim in the same direction, into the current set up by the filter, to get more oxygen.

Boat trips This was the first aquarium to have a department devoted to aquatic conservation. The *Voyager II* whalewatch trip is highly recommended, as is the 'Science at Sea' harbour tour, when you can haul lobster traps and tow for plankton.

BOSTON HARBOR ISLANDS

Gather wild raspberries, picnic on a beach, visit a ruined fort – all within sight of the city? These oases of wilderness are ringed by Boston, its airport and suburbs: it's just incredible they've escaped development.

America's newest national park Having played their part in history as defensive sites and home to prisons and poorhouses, the Boston Harbor Islands were largely ignored until they became a National Recreation Area (part of the National Park system) in 1996. People are only now beginning to appreciate these havens of wildlife, so near, yet so distant in feel.

Island hopping You can visit six of the 30 islands, and it's a 45-minute ferry ride from Long Wharf to Georges Island. From here two water taxis loop to Gallops and Lovells, and to Peddocks, Bumpkin and Grape. The islands are small, so you can visit more than one in a day; each has its own story, its own character. Georges attracts most visitors; on the others you may be all but alone. All have picnic areas (bring food and drink as there's no fresh water). Take guided walks, hike trails on your own or just beachcomb (beaches are mostly pebbly so wear protective shoes). Gallops and Lovells have sandy, supervised swimming beaches.

Something for everyone On Georges clamber over Fort Warren, where Civil War soldiers were imprisoned (find the hidden spiral staircase and get superb views of the city skyline). Peddocks and Lovells also have ruined forts. Bumpkin is where to pick those raspberries. Join myriad rabbits in the meadows on Gallops; study the wildlife in the rock pools, salt marsh, meadows and woodland on Peddocks. On Grape, crunch along beaches covered in iridescent blue mussel shells. All the islands are good for birdwatching.

HIGHLIGHTS

- The sense of escape
- Picnicking on a beach
- Fort Warren's dungeons
- Views of Boston skyline

INFORMATION

- ✚ Off map east at J4
- ✉ Boston Harbor Islands, National Park Service, 408 Atlantic Avenue, Boston, MA 02210-3350
- ☎ 617/223 8666
- 🕐 Georges Island May–mid-Oct: daily ferries (schedule ☎ 617/227 4321). The five other islands mid-Jun–Labor Day: daily. May–Jun, day after Labor Day–mid-Oct: Sat–Sun
- 🍴 Snack bar and barbecues on Georges. No drinking water on any islands. Take food and plenty to drink
- ⛴ Long Wharf to Georges Island. Water taxis from Georges to five other islands (see 🕐 above)
- ♿ Difficult
- 💵 Ferry expensive. Water taxi free
- 🔄 Faneuil Hall & Marketplace (➤ 42), New England Aquarium (➤ 46)
- ❓ Organised activities and tours. For lighthouse and occasional winter trips ☎ 781/740 4299

Wooded Grape Island with Boston's suburban skyline beyond

25

JOHN F KENNEDY LIBRARY & MUSEUM

HIGHLIGHTS

- The building, its setting and views
- Introductory video
- Oval Office

DID YOU KNOW?

- The library holds 8,400,000 JFK presidential papers

INFORMATION

- K9
- Columbia Point, Dorchester (Route 3/I-93 exit 15)
- 617/929 4500
- Daily 9–5
- Café on premises
- JFK/U Mass, then free shuttle bus
- Shuttle from Long Wharf, summer ☎ 617/929 4523
- Excellent
- Expensive. Boston CityPass applies
- Shop

'A man may die, nations may rise and fall, but an idea lives on,' said the late president John F Kennedy, whose life, leadership and legacy are brilliantly evoked in this dramatic modern museum by the sea.

The setting The presidential library and its museum, constructed in 1979, are housed in an I M Pei building on Dorchester Bay, 4 miles southeast of downtown Boston. The building's two towers, of dark glass and smooth white concrete, command fine views of the city, the bay and Boston Harbor Islands. The lawns, dune grass and wild roses on the grounds recall the Kennedy summer home on Cape Cod.

The New Museum An introductory film covers Kennedy's early years from childhood to the 1960 presidential campaign. Re-created settings include the White House corridors and the Oval Office, complete with the rocking chair JFK used for his bad back and, on his desk, the coconut inscribed 'HELP' that led to his rescue after his naval ship sank in the Pacific. Videos cover significant events such as the Cuban Missile Crisis, the space programme and the assassination. There are family photographs and other memorabilia and exhibits covering the life and work of First Lady Jacqueline Bouvier Kennedy.

The Presidential Library This is one of nine presidential libraries holding the papers of nine of the US presidents since Herbert Hoover. The Presidential Library System allows presidents to establish a library and museum where ever they choose. The JFK Library is near his mother's home.

BOSTON's
best

Neighbourhoods	*50–51*
Houses, Museums &	
Galleries	*52–53*
Buildings: Late 19th &	
20th Century	*54*
Statues, Monuments &	
Sculptures	*55*
Places of Worship & Burial	
Grounds	*56*
Parks & Retreats	*57*
Sports & Outdoor	
Activities	*58*
Things for Children	
to See & Do	*59*
Freebies & Cheapies	*60*

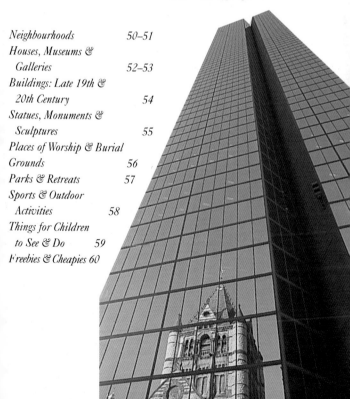

NEIGHBOURHOODS

See Top 25 Sights for
BACK BAY (▶ 33)
BEACON HILL (▶ 35)
THE NORTH END (▶ 44)

Chinatown

CAMBRIDGE

Cambridge is a town with its own character on the other side of the Charles River, but it is so accessible it feels like part of Boston. Home to Harvard, MIT and 28,000 students from all around the world, Cambridge is nothing if not vibrant. Life centres on several 'squares' or districts. There is lots for visitors to see and do in and around Harvard Square (▶ 25, 26), both by day and by night. Inman Square, Central Square and Porter Square all have a diversity of international restaurants. Kendall Square, MIT's home, close to the river and the CambridgeSide Galleria mall, also has a lively night scene. North of Cambridge, Somerville has a burgeoning number of good places to eat around Davis Square and Union Square.

CHINATOWN AND THE THEATER DISTRICT

Bounded by Washington Street, Essex Street, Kneeland Street and the Central Artery, between the Theater District and Financial District, Boston's Chinatown is not large but offers a real taste of Chinese daily life and Far Eastern cuisine. The principal artery is Beach Street, with the traditional gateway at the eastern end. With the Theater District on the other side of Washington Street, Chinatown is handy for late eating. Be aware that the area borders the Combat Zone – the (rapidly shrinking) red-light district along lower Washington Street.

DOWNTOWN CROSSING

Immediately east of Boston Common is a mostly pedestrianised shopping area that encompasses part of Washington Street and the streets that link it to Tremont Street. Department stores Filene's and Macy's are here, as well as Filene's Basement (▶ 72).

FENWAY

Art and sport meet here with the Museum of Fine Arts (▶ 28) and the Isabella Stewart Gardner Museum (▶ 27) on one side of the Back Bay Fens public park, and Fenway Park, home of the Red Sox and the Green Monster (▶ 58) on the other.

FINANCIAL DISTRICT AND LEATHER DISTRICT

The Financial District has some interesting buildings
(► 54). Between there and Chinatown, cornered by
Kneeland Street and Atlantic Avenue, is the Leather
District, a piece of 19th-century industrial
Boston whose redbrick buildings once
serviced the shoe industry and now house
offices and the occasional wine bar.

THE OLD WEST END
AND GOVERNMENT CENTER

Though not an exciting district, the old
West End has the FleetCenter, home to the
Celtics and Bruins (► 58), next to North
station. Beside the Charles River lies the
granite Old Jail and hidden in Massachusetts
General Hospital is the Bulfinch Pavilion,
where ether was first used as an anaesthetic.
Nearby, Cambridge Street, at the northern
foot of Beacon Hill, runs east to
Government Center and City Hall Plaza, an
impersonal area of office blocks ringed by
Beacon Hill, Faneuil and the North End.

THE SOUTH END

First occupied by musicians and teachers in
the 1850s and 1860s, the South End had
taken a social nosedive by the end of the
19th century but is now very much back in
favour with young professionals. It is a lively
residential area whose elegant bowfronted
terraces, many profusely decorated with
balustrades and window boxes, line leafy streets and
squares. Running through the middle is Tremont
Street, where local shops are punctuated by a growing
number of hip places to eat and shop. There is a
broad ethnic mix here and a strong gay element. Not
to be confused with South Boston, further to the east,
the South End lies between Huntington Avenue and
the Expressway. See panel for a walk.

WATERFRONT

The Waterfront, immediately east of Faneuil Hall
Marketplace, the North End and the Financial
District, is currently being ravaged by the
construction work that will bury the Central Artery.
Its old granite wharf buildings that once bustled with
commercial activity are now luxury condos or offices
overlooking trendy yacht havens. Boat trips leave
from Long Wharf, the Aquarium and Rowes Wharf
► 19, 46). A walkway runs along to Museum Wharf
► 59 for the Children's Museum) and there are
several seafood restaurants (► 64).

Ironwork typical of the South End

A South End stroll

From Copley or Back Bay T, walk
south down Dartmouth Avenue,
over Columbus Avenue. Zig-zag
through Lawrence, Appleton and
Gray streets. Take Clarendon Street
down to Tremont Street. Go right
and left into Union Park. Go right
(west) along Shawmut Avenue,
right onto Upton or Pembroke
Street. Left at Tremont, right onto
Rutland or Concord Square. Cut
back across Columbus Avenue and
up West Newton Street to
Huntington Avenue and the Pru T.

HOUSES, MUSEUMS & GALLERIES

Brookline sightseeing

JFK National Historic Site
➕ B5 ✉ 83 Beals Street
☎ 617/566 7937 🕐 Mid-Mar
to Nov: Wed–Sun 10–4:30
Ⓜ Coolidge Corner (green
line C)

**Frederick Law Olmsted
National Historic Site**
Landscaped gardens
➕ C8 ✉ 99 Warren Street
☎ 617/566 1689 🕐 Fri–Sun
10–4:30 Ⓜ Brookline Hills
(green line D) then ¾-mile walk.

Museum of Transportation
In Larz Anderson Park
➕ A10 ✉ 15 Newton Street,
Brookline ☎ 617/522 6547
🕐 Tue–Sun, Mon in hols 10–5
Ⓜ Cleveland Circle (green line
C), then bus 51 (not Sun)

*JFK's birthplace,
Brookline*

See Top 25 Sights for
HARRISON GRAY OTIS HOUSE (► 37)
HARVARD UNIVERSITY MUSEUMS (► 26)
ISABELLA STEWART GARDNER MUSEUM
(► 27)
JOHN F KENNEDY LIBRARY & MUSEUM
(► 48)
LONGFELLOW HOUSE (► 24)
MUSEUM OF FINE ARTS (► 28)
MUSEUM OF SCIENCE (► 34)
PAUL REVERE HOUSE (► 45)
USS *CONSTITUTION* MUSEUM (► 43)

**BOSTON TEA PARTY
SHIP & MUSEUM**
Board a replica Tea
Party ship, stick a
plastic feather in your
hair, boo the Brits and
maybe get to throw a
styrofoam tea chest
into the sea – but be
aware that there are
other ways of learning
about this significant
event (► 40).
➕ H5 ✉ Congress Street
Bridge ☎ 617/338 1773
🕐 Daily 9–5 (summer 9–6). Closed 1 Dec–Feb 🍴 Nearby Ⓜ South
station ♿ No wheelchair access to boat 💰 Expensive

CHILDREN'S MUSEUM (► 59)

GIBSON HOUSE MUSEUM
This 1860 Back Bay family home, with its opulent
furnishings and wonderful collection of Victoriana has
hardly been touched since it was built.
Complete with creaky stairs, it is a fragile
treasure worth fitting into your schedule if you
can. Afternoon tours only.
➕ G5 ✉ 137 Beacon Street ☎ 617/267 6338 🕐 For
tours only at 1, 2, 3PM. May–Oct: Wed–Sun. Nov–Apr: Sat,
Sun. Also by appointment Ⓜ Arlington ♿ No wheelchair
access 💰 Moderate

INSTITUTE OF CONTEMPORARY ART (ICA)
An exhibition, film and performance space
housed in a 19th-century police and fire
station. No permanent collection, but
whatever's on is likely to be innovative.
➕ F5 ✉ 955 Boylston Street (at Hereford Street)
☎ 617/267 5152 🕐 Wed–Sun noon–5 (Thu until 9)
Ⓜ Hynes Convention Center/ICA 💰 Moderate; free Thu 5–9

MIT MUSEUMS

The main MIT exhibition space has a unique collection of holograms, including one of a woman winking and blowing a kiss at you. It is also home to the Hall of Hacks, featuring MIT student pranks (on display is the police car found on top of the MIT Dome in May 1994). Flashes of Inspiration explores the work of MIT legend, Harold 'Doc' Edgerton who made the invisible visible. See his sequential photos of a balloon bursting. The Hart Nautical Collections, in the main campus, cover the technical side of naval architecture with exquisite ship models. The List Visual Art Center exhibits cutting edge work, including video and computer effects.

⊞ E4 ✉ 265 Massachusetts Avenue, Cambridge ☎ 617/253 4444 ◷ Tue–Fri 10–5; Sat, Sun noon–5 Ⓒ Central ▣ 1 to Necco Candy stop 💷 Inexpensive

Hart Nautical Gallery ⊞ E4 ✉ Building 5, 77 Massachusetts Avenue ☎ 617/253 5942 ◷ Daily 9–8 Ⓒ Kendall 💷 Free

List Visual Art Center ⊞ E4 ✉ 20 Ames Street, Cambridge ☎ 617/253 4400 ◷ Tue–Sun noon–6 (Fri until 8) Ⓒ Kendall 💷 Free

MUSEUM OF AFRO-AMERICAN HISTORY/AFRICAN MEETING HOUSE

A museum dedicated to the history of African Americans in Boston is housed in the African Meeting House, built in 1806 and the oldest surviving African-American church building in the US. Originally a centre for social and political activity, it is now a focal point on the Black Heritage Trail, a walking tour of pre-Civil War Beacon Hill sites including Smith Court Residences and Abiel Smith School.

⊞ B3 ✉ 46 Joy Street ☎ 617/739 1200 ◷ Memorial Day–Labor day: daily 10–4. Rest of year: Mon–Fri 10–4 Ⓒ Bowdoin 💷 Free

NICHOLS HOUSE MUSEUM

One of Boston's earliest Federal-style houses, this elegant four-storey Beacon Hill house was built by Charles Bulfinch (▶ 12, 35) in 1804 and is furnished with Nichols family art and antiques. The guide is informative, but also talkative.

⊞ B3 ✉ 55 Mount Vernon Street ☎ 617/227 6993 ◷ May–Oct: Tue–Sat noon–5. Nov, Dec; Feb–Apr: Mon, Wed, Sat noon–5. By tour only; last tour 4:15 Ⓒ Park Street 💷 Moderate

PHOTOGRAPHIC RESOURCE CENTER

Good exhibition for photography buffs – in the basement of a Boston University building.

⊞ D5 ✉ 602 Commonwealth Avenue ☎ 617/353 0700 ◷ Tue–Sun noon–5 (Thu until 8) Ⓒ Boston University East 💷 Inexpensive

Harold Edgerton's Milkdrop Coronet *in his* Flashes of Inspiration *exhibit at MIT Museum*

BUILDINGS: LATE 19TH CENTURY & 20TH CENTURY

> **See Top 25 Sights for**
> **BOSTON PUBLIC**
> **LIBRARY (► 31)**
> **JOHN HANCOCK**
> **TOWER (► 30)**
> **TRINITY CHURCH (► 32)**

AMES AND SEARS BUILDINGS

The highly decorative 14-storey 1889 Ames Building at the back of the Old State House dominated the skyline until the Custom House Tower was built. The nearby Sears Building (1868) was the first in the city to have an elevator.
✚ dIII; H4 ✉ 1 Court Street
Ⓜ State

CUSTOM HOUSE TOWER

The square clock tower (1915) is a Boston landmark and at 30 storeys was for a long while the city's tallest skyscraper. It's only when you see the building at street level that you realise how ridiculous it looks stuck on the roof of the original Custom House, built in 1847 like a temple, in Greek Revival style. The clock faces are notorious for showing different times.
✚ dIII; H4 ✉ State Street Ⓜ State

Downtown, near State Street

MIT Buildings

MIT has some impressive modern architecture. You are free to wander around the campus. Seek out Eero Saarinen's serene round chapel (1955), near the Student Center on Massachusetts Avenue. Overlooking the river nearby, the student dorm Baker House (1947) is by Finnish architect Alvar Aalto, while on and near Ames Street the low Wiesner and the tall Green buildings are the work of I M Pei (1964, 1985).
✚ E4 ✉ Massachusetts Avenue, Memorial Drive, Ames Street Ⓜ Kendall

IN AND AROUND POST OFFICE SQUARE

On the corner of Water and Congress, note the elaborate façade of the art deco US Post Office and Court House (1931). Next to it is Arts & Crafts at 79 Milk Street, with green and white detailing at roof level, and at the south end of the square is the striking New England Telephone building. In Franklin Street find good art deco metal-work on the exterior walls of the State Street Trust Building at 75, and in the foyer of State Street Bank, No. 225. Worthy of mention, too, are the stepped-back United Shoe Machinery building (1929), 138–164 Federal Street at High Street and the 1928 Batterymarch building at 60 Batterymarch Street.

WINTHROP BUILDING

Boston's first all steel-framed skyscraper (1894).
✚ dIV; H5 ✉ 7 Water Street, between Washington Street and Post Office Square Ⓜ State

STATUES, MONUMENTS & SCULPTURES

See Top 25 Sights for
COMMONWEALTH AVENUE (▶ 33)
THE PUBLIC GARDEN (▶ 36)

SAM ADAMS
Anne Whitney's (1880) portrayal of the defiant revolutionary leader, in front of Faneuil Hall.
🔟 dIII; H4 ✉ Congress Street 🚇 State

BUNKER HILL MONUMENT
The Charlestown skyline is punctuated by this plain grey obelisk commemorating the revolutionary Battle of Bunker Hill. Climb 274 steps for good views.
🔟 H2 ✉ Monument Square, Charlestown ☎ 617/242 5641 🕐 Monument daily 9–4:30. Base lodge (toy soldier battle display) daily 9–5 🚢 Long Wharf to Charlestown 🚇 Community College 🆓 Free

JAMES CURLEY
A colourful Boston Irish mayor, Curley (1874–1958) comes seated and standing (Lloyd Lillie, 1980).
🔟 dIII; H4 ✉ North/Union Street 🚇 State

MAKE WAY FOR DUCKLINGS (▶ 59)

MIT SCULPTURES
On the campus are two Henry Moore reclining figure pieces (1963, 1976), Alexander Calder's black steel *The Big Sail* (1965) and Michael Heizer's pink granite *Guennette* (1977).
🔟 E4 ✉ Memorial Drive 🕐 Daily 🚇 Kendall 🆓 Free

NEW ENGLAND HOLOCAUST MEMORIAL
Six glass towers, the poignant work of Stanley Saitowitz (1995), recall Nazi death camps. Etched numerals represent the Holocaust's 6 million victims.
🔟 dIII; H4 ✉ Union Street 🚇 State

PAUL REVERE
A bronze equestrian statue (1940) of the legendary figure (▶ 12) by Cyrus Dallin.
🔟 dII; H4 ✉ Paul Revere Mall, North End 🚇 State, Aquarium, North station

ROBERT GOULD SHAW MONUMENT
A sensitive bronze battle frieze by Augustus Saint-Gaudens (1897). Shaw, depicted in the film *Glory*, led the Union's first black regiment off to battle in the Civil War. Here, for the first time, blacks were portrayed by a white artist as individuals.
🔟 bIV; G4 ✉ Beacon Street, facing State House 🚇 Park

Art on the T
MBTA (Massachusetts Bay Transportation Authority) has an enlightened policy of installing works of art in its underground stations. Keep an eye out, for example, for the layered hands sculpture and the ceramic mural in Park Street station, the granite benches placed randomly on the platforms at Downtown Crossing or the multicoloured 'Omphaios' sculpture outside Harvard Square station.

Statue of Paul Revere

55

PLACES OF WORSHIP & BURIAL GROUNDS

See Top 25 Sights for
FIRST CHURCH OF CHRIST, SCIENTIST (► 29)
OLD NORTH CHURCH (► 44)
OLD SOUTH MEETING HOUSE (► 40)
TRINITY CHURCH (► 32)

AFRICAN MEETING HOUSE (► 53)

Mount Auburn Cemetery, Cambridge

A little out of the way, but a beautiful place. It was built in 1831 as the country's first rural garden cemetery and is still very popular with bird and plant lovers. If it's a nice day you could walk from Longfellow's House (► 24). Longfellow now rests here, as does artist Winslow Homer.

➕ 2B ✉ Mount Auburn Street, Cambridge ☎ 617/547 7105 🕐 Daily 🚇 Harvard, then walk or Watertown bus

Park Street Church

COPP'S HILL BURYING GROUND
Up on top of an old Native American lookout point in the North End, the rows of carved skulls have good all-round views. Puritans Increase and Cotton Mather are buried here.

➕ dl; H3 ✉ Hull Street 🕐 Daily 🚇 North station

KING'S CHAPEL AND BURYING GROUND
This was built as an Anglican church in 1687 on the orders of King James II, to the indignation of the Puritan colonists. In the town's earliest (1630) burial ground lie two *Mayflower* passengers and John Winthrop, first governor of Massachusetts.

➕ clV; H4 ✉ Tremont/School streets 🚇 Park

OLD GRANARY BURYING GROUND
If you can take in only one burial ground, make it this one. Dating back to 1660, it's the leafy resting place of many of the big names you keep coming across – Paul Revere, James Otis, John Hancock, Samuel Adams, Peter Faneuil. A board tells you about the wonderful carvings on the headstones.

➕ clV; H5 ✉ 88 Tremont Street 🕐 Daily 🚇 Park

PARK STREET CHURCH
Notable as much for its tall white steeple as for William Lloyd Garrison's first anti-slavery speech made in 1829. 'America the Beautiful' was first sung here in 1831.

➕ clV; H5 ✉ 1 Park Street 🕐 Jul–Aug: daily 🚇 Park

ST STEPHEN'S CHURCH
Of the dozen churches Charles Bulfinch designed for post-Independence Boston, this is the only one still standing (1804). Its redbrick tower contrasts with the wide, white-painted Federal interior.

➕ E15 ✉ 41 Hanover Street 🕐 Daily 🚇 State

PARKS & RETREATS

See Top 25 Sights for
THE PUBLIC GARDEN (► 36)
BOSTON COMMON (► 36)
BOSTON HARBOR ISLANDS (► 47)

ARNOLD ARBORETUM
Stunning in all seasons, this is a rolling hilly park
that's well worth the trip to the suburbs. Part of
Olmsted's Emerald Necklace (see panel).
🔲 B10 ✉ 125 Arborway, Jamaica Plain ☎ 617/524 1718
🚇 Orange line to Forest Hills 🎟 Free

BACK BAY FENS
The Back Bay Fens was the first of Olmsted's string
of parks (see panel). Tall rushes line the Muddy
River banks behind the Museum of Fine Arts;
people stroll through the willows and sit in the Rose
Garden.
🔲 E6 ✉ The Fenway/Park Drive 🚇 Museum, Hynes

CHARLES RIVER: ESPLANADE AND BOAT TOURS
A favourite for roller blading, jogging, sunbathing and
more (► 58 biking, boating); free summer concerts in
Hatch Memorial Shell (► 78); you can also watch
open-air film screenings here. Charles River Boat
Tours leave from CambridgeSide near the Science
Museum.
Esplanade 🔲 F5 ✉ Storrow Memorial Drive 🚇 Charles/MGH
Riverboat Tours 🔲 B10 ✉ 100 CambridgeSide ☎ 617/621
3001 🕐 Memorial Day–Labor Day: daily. Apr, May, Oct: Sat, Sun
🚇 Science Park

CHRISTOPHER COLUMBUS PARK
This is a small park not far from Faneuil Hall
Marketplace (follow the harbourwalk signs under the
expressway). It's right on the waterfront and good for
watching the comings and goings of boats in the
harbour and planes at Logan.
🔲 H4 ✉ Atlantic Avenue 🚇 Aquarium

The Emerald Necklace

So called because it resembles a
string of beads, Boston's
interconnecting chain of parks
was designed in 1895, when such
things were a novel idea, by
America's first landscape architect,
Frederick Law Olmsted. The
gardens of Commonwealth
Avenue link Boston Common and
the Public Garden with the Back
Bay Fens. From here it is possible
to walk along the reed-fringed
Riverway to Olmsted Park and on
to Jamaica Pond, a popular spot
for fishing and boating. Arnold
Arboretum (see left) is ½ mile
away and then there's Franklin
Park, with a zoo (► 59).

*Autumn colours on the
Charles River Esplanade*

SPORT & OUTDOOR ACTIVITIES

Sailing on the Charles River

The major venues

Fenway Park ✚ E6 ✉ 24
Yawkey Way ☎ 617/267 8661
🚇 Kenmore Square

FleetCenter ✚ cl; H4 ✉ 150
Causeway Street ☎ 617/624
1000 🚇 North station

Tickets

Ticketmaster ☎ 617/931
2000/2787 or at **BosTix** stalls in
Faneuil Hall Marketplace, Copley
Square and Holyoke Center in
Harvard Square (➤ 80)
Bruins ☎ 617/931 2020
(ticketmaster) or in person at
FleetCenter box office
Celtics ☎ 617/523 3030 or in
person at FleetCenter box office
Red Sox ☎ 617/267 1700 or
in person at Fenway Park box
office
US Pro Tennis ☎ Ticketmaster
(see above)

BASEBALL/FENWAY TOURS
The beloved Boston Red Sox play at Fenway Park from April to October. Aged, cramped and idiosyncratic, Fenway is famous for its Green Monster – the unusually high left field wall, but there are plans to replace Fenway with a new ballpark in the near future.

BASKETBALL
The Boston Celtics play October to May in the FleetCenter.

BIKING, IN-LINE SKATING AND JOGGING
The Esplanade is always popular. On spring and summer Sundays Memorial Drive, on the Cambridge side of the river, is closed to vehicles, so you can walk, cycle or skate along one bank, cross on any bridge and return on the other. For bicycle and in-line skate rental (➤ 74, panel).

BOATING
Canoes, kayaks and sailing dinghies can be rented at the Charles River Esplanade.

THE BOSTON MARATHON
Started in 1897, the first marathon in the US and the world's oldest annual event, this 26.2-mile run (Hopkinton to Copley Square) takes place the third Monday in April (Patriots' Day).

HEAD OF THE CHARLES REGATTA
Thousands come, often with picnics, for this major international rowing event in October.

ICE HOCKEY
The NHL's illustrious Boston Bruins play at FleetCenter (October to April). The Beanpot inter-collegiate tournament is held in early February.

SKATING
In winter join the ritual skating on Frog Pond on Boston Common. Rent skates from kiosk.
☎ 617/635 2120

US PRO TENNIS TOURNAMENT
The tournament is held in the third or fourth week of August at the Longwood Cricket Club in Brookline.
☎ 617/731 2900 🚇 Chestnut Hill (green line D)

THINGS FOR CHILDREN TO SEE & DO

See Top 25 Sights for
BOSTON HARBOR ISLANDS (► 47)
MUSEUM OF SCIENCE (► 34)
NEW ENGLAND AQUARIUM (► 46)
USS *CONSTITUTION* MUSEUM (► 43)

Children love the street performers in Faneuil Marketplace, and there are gift shops, confectionery stalls and food stands. Harvard Square, too, has plenty of entertainment. Whalewatching trips, Duck Tours and Swan Boats (► 46, 19, 36) are popular, as are the John Hancock Observatory and/or Prudential Skywalk (► 30) and the Mapparium (► 29). The museums and galleries often have activities laid on for children; the programmes at the Museum of Fine Arts (► 28) are particularly well recommended.

BOSTON TEA PARTY SHIP & MUSEUM (► 52)

CHILDREN'S MUSEUM
This museum is heaven on earth for the under-10s – and it's expanding into the former Computer Museum's site next door. Try the new balance climb, play at shops with life-size products, squirt water jets at model boats, stretch a gigantic bubble or just have fun in the playspace. And when you're all exhausted, retreat to the peace and quiet of the Japanese house.
⊞ J5 ⊠ 300 Congress Street, Museum Wharf ☎ 617/426 8855 ⏰ Mid-Jun to Labor Day: daily 10–5 (Fri until 9). Sep–Jun: closed Mon except school and public hols 🍴 McDonald's adjoins 🚇 South station 💵 Expensive. Fri 5–9 $1

FRANKLIN PARK ZOO
Wander through an African Tropical Forest, stroke small animals at the Children's Zoo, visit the lions, then picnic in the park's meadows.
⊞ E10 ⊠ 1 Franklin Park Road ☎ 617/442 2002 ⏰ Daily 🍴 Café or picnic 🚇 Forest Hills (orange line) then bus 16 💵 Moderate; under 4 free

MIT MUSEUMS (► 53)

PLIMOTH PLANTATION (► 21)

PUPPET THEATER (► 80–81)

Playgrounds
There are good playgrounds where young children can let off steam: on the Boston Common, on the Charles River Esplanade, in the Waterfront Columbus Park (not far from the Aquarium), in Clarendon Street in the South End and on Cambridge Common.

'Make way for ducklings'
Look out for the mother duck and ducklings in the Public Garden, a bronze sculpture based on Robert McCloskey's famous book. The same artist, Nancy Schon, created the hare and tortoise who mark the spot where the Boston Marathon ends in Copley Square.

Make way for ducklings!

FREEBIES & CHEAPIES

A Boston Pops concert in the Hatch Shell

Places of interest with free entry

African Meeting House (➤ 53)

Boston Public Library (➤ 31)

Bunker Hill Monument (➤ 55)

Charlestown Navy Yard Ships and Museum (➤ 43)

First Church of Christ, Scientist, Mapparium and Mother Church (➤ 29)

Commonwealth Museum, history and people of Massachusetts ✉ 220 Morrissey Boulevard, Columbia Point ☎ 617/727 9268 ⏰ Mon–Fri 9–5; Sat 9–3

Faneuil Hall (➤ 42)

Harvard University Museums (➤ 26) ⏰ Wed all day and Sat AM.

Massachusetts State House (➤ 38)

MIT's List Visual Art Center and Hart Nautical Galleries (➤ 53)

Trinity Church (and free organ recitals Fri 12:15 ➤ 32)

Street entertainment

Harvard Square in Cambridge and Faneuil Hall Marketplace in Boston are both excellent places to catch street performers and for people-watching.

SPECIAL ADMISSION CHARGES

Several places offer reduced-price or free entry at certain times. The Museum of Fine Arts is pay-as-you-wish Wednesday 4–9:45. Harvard University Museums are free all day Wednesday and Saturday 10–noon. The ICA is free Thursday 5–9. Admission to the Children's Museum is $1 Friday 5–9.

FESTIVALS

From summer festivals in the Italian North End and 4th of July fireworks displays on the Esplanade to the First Night celebrations on New Year's Eve, there's nearly always some free event going on. Check the *Boston Globe* or *Phoenix*.

MUSICAL ENTERTAINMENT

The ever-popular Boston Pops orchestra holds free concerts in July in the Hatch Memorial Shell on the Esplanade (➤ 78). Concerts at the New England Conservatory are free (➤ 78, January to March). The Boston Symphony Orchestra has inexpensive open rehearsals. See the *Boston Globe* or *Phoenix*. Trinity Church (➤ 79) holds free organ recitals Fridays 12:15. The Federal Reserve Bank of Boston hosts free concerts at noon.
✉ 600 Atlantic Avenue (opposite South station) ☎ 617/913 3453

PARKS AND OPEN SPACES

It doesn't cost anything to enjoy the places described under Parks and Retreats (➤ 57). Boston Common, the Public Garden and the Esplanade are year-round favourites. Public spaces all over the city are notably rich in sculptures, murals and other art installations.

BOSTON
where to...

EAT

The Best of Boston	*62–63*
Seafood	*64*
Italian & Mediterranean	*65*
American & Mexican	*66*
Asian & Middle Eastern	*67*
Brunch, Coffee, Tea &	
Late Eating	*68–69*

SHOP

Districts & Department	
Stores	*70–71*
Clothes	*72–73*
Shoes & Outdoor Gear	*74*
Books, Maps & Music	*75*
Crafts, Gifts & Household	
Goods	*76–77*

BE ENTERTAINED

Classical Music, Opera &	
Dance	*78–79*
Theatre & Cinema	*80–81*
Clubs & Bars	*82–83*

STAY

Luxury Hotels	*84*
Mid-Range Hotels	*85*
Budget Accommodation	*86*

THE BEST OF BOSTON

Prices

Approximate prices for a two-course meal for one with a drink:

£	up to $18
££	up to $35
£££	more than $35

Boston classics

Timeless institutions include:

Durgin Park

One of the oldest dining rooms in the US. The roast beef melts in the mouth and there's hard-to-find traditional fare like Indian pudding. Crowded; very informal – but the waiters make a thing of being rude.

✉ Faneuil Hall Marketplace
☎ 617/227 2038

Locke-Ober Café

Originally a gentlemen's club, and still feels like one. Old-fashioned, but competently executed menu.

✉ 3 Winter Place
☎ 617/542 1340
🕐 Closed Sun

Ritz-Carlton

Formal dining under the chandeliers of the elegant room overlooking the Public Garden. Outstanding service and food.

✉ 15 Arlington Street
☎ 617/536 5700

AMBROSIA ON HUNTINGTON (£££)

The unconventional menu at this hip, postmodern spot blends French, Italian and Asian in bold new dishes: try the Japonaise roasted duck with fig-stilton glaze.

✚ F6 ✉ 116 Huntington Avenue ☎ 617/247 2400 🕐 Mon–Fri lunch; daily dinner 🚇 Prudential

AUJOURD'HUI (£££)

Overlooking the Public Garden and known as much for the service as the food, this is one of Boston's very best formal restaurants. The chef's complex presentations and unusual combinations are pricey, but overall, it's close to perfect.

✚ G5 ✉ Four Seasons Hotel, 200 Boylston Street ☎ 617/451 1392 🕐 Mon–Fri lunch; daily dinner; Sun brunch 🚇 Arlington

BIBA (£££)

Perhaps Boston's most famous chef, Lydia Shire is revered for her rich and satisfying personal style of cooking. On the unusually arranged menu – dishes are listed by principal ingredients rather than category – offal plays a special role. The upstairs room has views of the Public Garden. Less formal eating at the bar.

✚ G5 ✉ 272 Boylston Street ☎ 617/426 7878 🕐 Mon–Fri lunch; daily dinner; Sun brunch 🚇 Arlington

CAFÉ BUDAPEST (£££)

Romantic Hungarian restaurant in something of a time warp – violins and

all. Good service. Soups are a speciality. Dressy.

✚ F5 ✉ Copley Square Hotel, 90 Exeter Street ☎ 617/266 1979, 617/734 3388 🕐 Mon–Sat lunch; daily dinner 🚇 Copley

CHEZ HENRI (£££)

Trendy French/Cuban. Service can be tardy, but it's worth the wait; food is uniformly wonderful: try crispy cod cakes with crab-avocado salsa.

✚ C2 ✉ 1 Shepard Street at Massachusetts Avenue ☎ 617/354 8980 🕐 Daily dinner; Sun brunch 🚇 Harvard then bus 77 or walk

CLIO (£££)

Excellent contemporary fare that's creative without being weird. A fine choice for business entertaining. The leopard-print rug adds just the right level of 'chic' to an otherwise sedate dining room. Good seafood preparations including crispy Ipswich clams and butter-basted lobster with lemon foam.

✚ E5 ✉ Eliot Hotel, 370a Commonwealth Avenue ☎ 617/536 7200 🕐 Daily dinner; Sun brunch 🚇 Hynes/ICA

THE ELEPHANT WALK (££)

Intriguing Cambodian and French food. Very popular with students and young trendies. Locations:

✚ D6 ✉ 900 Beacon Street ☎ 617/247 1500 🕐 Mon–Sat lunch; daily dinner 🚇 St Mary's Street (green line C)

✚ Off map at 1C ✉ 2067 Massachusetts Avenue, Cambridge ☎ 617/492 6900 🕐 As above 🚇 Porter, then walk

HAMERSLEY'S BISTRO (£££)

Excellent American-French cooking in a pleasant, informal setting. Refreshingly simple preparations such as grilled beef tenderloin with roasted oysters.

✚ G6 ✉ 553 Tremont Street (at Clarendon) ☎ 617/423 2700 ◷ Dinner ⊜ Back Bay

JULIEN (£££)

Very French, very formal, very pricey, but superb. Not for those easily intimidated by the rituals of fine dining or those with an aversion to butter.

✚ dIV; H4 ✉ Le Meridien Hotel, 250 Franklin Street ☎ 617/451 1900 ◷ Mon–Fri lunch; Mon–Sat dinner ⊜ State, Downtown Crossing

LA BETTOLA (£££)

An unprepossessing storefront dining room. Excellent creative food – Italian-inspired, with an Asian sensibility. Try the wolf-fish lasagne layered with prosciutto and fennel.

✚ F6 ✉ 480a Columbus Avenue ☎ 617/236 5252 ◷ Dinner ⊜ Massachusetts Avenue, Prudential

L'ESPALIER (£££)

Superb contemporary fare in the formal and romantic setting of a 19th-century Back Bay house. Prix fixe.

✚ F5 ✉ 30 Gloucester Street ☎ 617/262 3023 ◷ Mon–Sat dinner ⊜ Hynes/ICA

MAISON ROBERT (££–£££)

As French as the name, the food at this Boston mainstay is good, if old-fashioned; the wine list impressive, if expensive.

✚ cIV; H4 ✉ 45 School Street ☎ 617/227 3370 ◷ Lunch; dinner ⊜ State, Park Street

NO. 9 PARK (£££)

New American fare in a dignified if simple dining room. Chef Barbara Lynch has a way with duck; her signature 'crispy duck' is deliciously crisp outside, meltingly tender within. Cheaper bar/café menu.

✚ bIV; G4 ✉ 9 Park Street ☎ 617/742 9991 ◷ Mon–Fri lunch; Mon–Sat dinner ⊜ Park

OLIVES (£££)

Inventive Mediterranean-influenced cooking; bold flavours, huge portions. Chef Todd English is a gossip-column favourite.

✚ H3 ✉ 10 City Square, Charlestown ☎ 617/242 1999 ◷ Mon–Sat dinner ⊜ North station, then walk; Haymarket, then bus 92 or 93

RADIUS (£££)

Culinary hotspot set in a 1920s one-time downtown bank. Chef Michael Schlow serves modern French: seared salmon with lentils, smoked bacon and spiced jus.

✚ H5 ✉ 8 High Street ☎ 617/426 2576 ◷ Mon–Fri lunch; Mon–Sat dinner ⊜ South station

RIALTO (£££)

A seasonal Mediterranean menu includes updated French and Italian classics as well as modern dishes.

✚ C3 ✉ Charles Hotel, 1 Bennett Street, Cambridge ☎ 617/661 5050 ◷ Dinner ⊜ Harvard

Hot districts

Boston's hottest restaurant district is the South End. And keep an eye on Somerville, north of Cambridge. In the South End:

Aquitaine

Popular upmarket French bistro and wine bar.

✉ 569 Tremont Street

☎ 617/424 8577

Truc

Tiny spot; creative French cuisine.

✉ 560 Tremont Street

☎ 617/338 8070

Tremont 647

Adventurous new American/fusion food; casually hip room. 'Pajama Brunch' on Sunday.

✉ 647 Tremont Street

☎ 617/266 4600

In Somerville:

The Burren

Davis Square Irish pub. Good fish and chips. Music on several nights.

✉ 247 Elm Street

☎ 617/776 6896

Rauxa

Catalan cuisine with an emphasis on seafood dishes.

✉ 70 Union Square

☎ 617/623 9939

Eat

Updated American classics in a small, unadorned room.

✉ 253 Washington Street

☎ 617/776 2889

SEAFOOD

More seafood options

Nowadays some of Boston's finest fish is served outside of the traditional seafood restaurants listed on this page. Most of the city's best eating spots do an excellent job with seafood preparations, and these dishes are taking an increasingly large share of their menus.

Other good choices for fresh seafood are any of the Chinatown restaurants with live-from-the-tanks fish preparations.

For landlubbers only: how to eat a lobster

1 Put the bib on.

2 Break the claws off.

3 Use the nutcracker to open them.

4 Bend the back until the tailpiece splits off.

5 Break the flippers off the tail.

6 Push the meat out of the tail with the thin fork.

7 Pull the back out of the body. You may not want to eat the liver.

8 Crack open the rest of the body sideways (the best meat is here).

9 Suck the meat out of the little claw.

ANTHONY'S PIER 4 (££)

Big, busy restaurant on the Fish Pier with spectacular downtown and harbour views. Traditional (if unexciting) seafood; stick to the classics. Jackets advisable.

➕ J5 ✉ 140 Northern Avenue ☎ 617/423 6363 ⏰ From 11:30; Sun from noon 🚇 South station

BARKING CRAB (£)

A rough and ready old clam shack where you can eat your fish and chips or fried clams indoors or alfresco, with downtown views of Boston across the water. Expect crowds, noise, a wait and fun.

➕ J5 ✉ 88 Sleeper Street, off Northern Avenue ☎ 617/426 2722 ⏰ From 11:30 🚇 South station

EAST COAST GRILL & RAW BAR (££–£££)

Wildly popular Inman Square seafood and barbecue joint. Fresh seafood often served with intriguing spice rubs and fruit salsas. Spicy food fans should try anything labeled 'from hell'. Booking Sunday to Thursday for parties of five or more.

➕ E3 ✉ 1272 Cambridge Street ☎ 617/491 6568 ⏰ Daily dinner; Sun brunch 🚇 Central, then long walk or bus 83 to Inman Square; Harvard then bus 69 on Cambridge Street

JIMMY'S HARBORSIDE (££)

Fine old institution – good fish and solid steak dishes, a first-class wine list and excellent waterfront views.

➕ J5 ✉ 242 Northern Avenue ☎ 617/423 1000 ⏰ From noon; Sun dinner 🚇 South station

LEGAL SEA FOODS (££)

Popular seafood chain serving straightforward, reliably good fish. Makes a decent clam chowder.

✉ 255 State Street; 26 Park Plaza; Prudential Center; Copley Plaza; 5 Cambridge Center, Kendall Square ☎ 617/742 5300; 617/426 4444; 617/266 6800; 617/266 7775; 617/864 3400 ⏰ Hours vary 🚇 Aquarium, Arlington, Prudential, Copley

SKIPJACK'S (££)

Well-prepared fish in comfortable surroundings. Lobster is a speciality, or try blackened tuna sashimi.

➕ F5 ✉ 199 Clarendon Street ☎ 617/536 3500 ⏰ From 11. Sun jazz brunch 🚇 Copley

TURNER FISHERIES (££)

The acclaimed seafood restaurant in the Westin Hotel prides itself on its clam chowder, so this has to be your benchmark. Good Sunday brunch. Live jazz next door.

➕ F5 ✉ The Westin Hotel, Copley Place, 10 Huntington Avenue ☎ 617/424 7425 ⏰ Mon–Sat lunch; daily dinner; Sun brunch from 11 🚇 Copley

UNION OYSTER HOUSE (££)

Said to be the oldest restaurant in the US; on the Freedom Trail. Boston scrod is a local favourite.

➕ dlll; H4 ✉ 41 Union Street ☎ 617/227 2750 ⏰ From 11 🚇 State, Government Center

ITALIAN & MEDITERRANEAN

ARTÙ (£)
Country-style Italian cooking in the North End. Friendly and informal. Try chicken layered with aubergine and mozzarella. Also at 89 Charles Street.

dll; H4 ⊠ 6 Prince Street ☎ 617/742 4336 ⊙ From 11 ⊙ Haymarket

CANTINA ITALIANA (£)
A relaxed North End eatery serving excellent regional Italian food.

dll; H4 ⊠ 346 Hanover Street ☎ 617/723 4577 ⊙ Mon–Sat from 4; Sun from noon ⊙ Haymarket

GALLERIA ITALIANA (££–£££)
Hidden away one block from the Theater District, this small room serves fine contemporary Italian fare (chicken breast with white polenta in an anise-grape sauce). Very busy pre-theatre, so come after 8PM.

G5 ⊠ 177 Tremont Street ☎ 617/423 2092 ⊙ Mon–Fri lunch; Tue–Sat dinner ⊙ Boylston

MAMMA MARIA (£££)
Highly regarded elegant North End Italian, offering imaginative cooking and gracious service with prices to match. Try the osso buco (traditional shin of veal stew).

dll; H4 ⊠ 3 North Square ☎ 617/523 0077 ⊙ Daily dinner ⊙ Haymarket

MARCUCCIO'S (£££)
Contemporary Italian fare in a funky North End storefront. Charles Draghi uses fresh vegetable broth or reductions instead of cream or butter, for lighter but still lusty dishes (wild striped bass in a lemon, olive oil and herb broth).

dll; H4 ⊠ 125 Salem Street ☎ 617/723 1807 ⊙ Daily dinner ⊙ Haymarket

PIGNOLI (£–££)
Inventive Italian-inspired cooking. Try the zuppa di pesce (fish soup) or the roasted beet ravioli with duck confit. Eclectic decor with huge paper lanterns.

G5 ⊠ 91 Park Plaza ☎ 617/338 7500 ⊙ Mon–Sat lunch; daily dinner 5:30–10 (Fri, Sat until 11) ⊙ Arlington

RISTORANTE TOSCANO (£££)
One of the best, this is an elegant eatery with a genuine Italian ambience. Try the risotto. Excellent wine list.

aIV; G4 ⊠ 47 Charles Street ☎ 617/723 4090 ⊙ Lunch, dinner ⊙ Charles/MGH

TAPEO (££)
Surreal Spanish restaurant and tapas bar very popular with the Gen X crowd. Be prepared to wait.

F5 ⊠ 266 Newbury Street ☎ 617/267 4799 ⊙ Sat, Sun lunch; daily dinner ⊙ Hynes/ICA

UPSTAIRS AT THE PUDDING (£££)
Northern Italy meets New England in this romantic restaurant above Harvard's Hasty Pudding Club Theater (butternut squash 'pasta pillow'). Eat in the rooftop garden in summer.

C3 ⊠ 10 Holyoke Street, Cambridge ☎ 617/864 1933 ⊙ Mon–Sat lunch; daily dinner; Sun brunch ⊙ Harvard

Dining with a view

Bay Tower Room
Look down on the city and harbour from 33 floors up. New American cuisine.

⊠ 60 State Street
☎ 617/723 1666

Joe's American Bar & Grill
Regional American dishes right on the water's edge.

⊠ 100 Atlantic Avenue
☎ 617/367 8700

Seasons
Luxury rooftop with views over Faneuil; new American cuisine.

⊠ Regal Bostonian Hotel, Faneuil Hall Marketplace
☎ 617/523 4149

Top of the Hub
The highest dining room in Boston, on the 52nd floor of the Prudential Tower. The scintillating night-time views are matched by the food. Also light (and less expensive) meals served in the lounge till Inte.

⊠ Prudential Center, Huntington Avenue
☎ 617/536 1775

Also worth trying: Aujourd'hui, Biba (both ► 62); Anthony's Pier 4, Barking Crab (► 64); Skyline, Museum of Science (► 68)

AMERICAN & MEXICAN

New England specialities

Try these: lobster, clam chowder, scrod, *quahog* (a large clam, pronounced 'ko hog'), Boston baked beans (cooked long and slow in an earthenware pot), Boston cream pie (chocolate-covered and custard-filled), Indian pudding (cornmeal, milk and molasses cooked long and slow).

Beer here!

Brewpubs are popping up all over Boston. Try:

Back Bay Brewing Company
✉ 755 Boylston Street, Back Bay ☎ 617/424 8300
Samuel Adams Brewhouse
✉ 710 Boylston Street, Back Bay ☎ 617/536 2739
Brew Moon
Popular, local mini-chain with better-than-average food to accompany their house-made beers.
✉ 115 Stuart Street, Theater District ☎ 617/523 6467;
✉ 50 Church Street (in the Atrium Building), Cambridge ☎ 617/499 2739

AMERICAN

GRILL 23 & BAR (£££)
Steaks of all kinds, plus prime rib of beef, lamb chops, swordfish and more. Attentive service in a beautiful dining room. Popular and noisy.
✚ G5 ✉ 161 Berkeley Street (at Stuart Street) ☎ 617/542 2255 ⏰ Dinner only ⓜ Arlington

HENRIETTA'S TABLE (££)
This country kitchen-style restaurant – a favourite of cooking legend Julia Child – provides creative New England food matched with an all-American wine list.
✚ C3 ✉ Charles Hotel, 1 Bennett Street, Cambridge ☎ 617/661 5005 ⏰ Breakfast, lunch, dinner; Sun brunch ⓜ Harvard Square

HUNGRY I (£££)
Tiny, intimate basement offering a small but inventive menu.
✚ aIV; G4 ✉ 71 Charles Street ☎ 617/227 3524 ⏰ Dinner; Sun brunch ⓜ Charles Street

ICARUS (£££)
Pleasant for a quiet meal in an elegant setting. Excellent contemporary cooking (oven-roasted crab cake with curry and cucumber); good wine list.
✚ G6 ✉ 3 Appleton Street ☎ 617/426 1790 ⏰ Dinner ⓜ Back Bay

METROPOLIS CAFÉ (£)
A South End local; honest contemporary food, (roast halibut with celery root puree; pork chop with crispy sage and mascarpone polenta).
✚ G6 ✉ 584 Tremont Street ☎ 617/247 2931 ⏰ Tue–Sun dinner; Sat, Sun brunch 9–3 ⓜ Back Bay

REDBONES (£)
A down-and-dirty rib joint, serving some of the area's best barbecued ribs. Excellent fried okra appetiser. Often crowded and boisterous. Interesting microbrews on tap.
✚ Off map at C1 ✉ 55 Chester Street at Elm Street, Somerville ☎ 617/628 2200 ⏰ Lunch, dinner ⓜ Davis

OAK ROOM (£££)
Dark oak-panelled walls and well-spaced tables make for club-like privacy in the grand dame of Boston's hotels. It's a steak house – but the lobster bouillabaisse is also superb.
✚ F5 ✉ Fairmount Copley Plaza Hotel, Copley Square ☎ 617/267 5300 ⏰ Dinner ⓜ Copley

MEXICAN

BORDER CAFÉ (£)
This frenetic eatery is one of the best Tex-Mex places in Cambridge. Very popular with students.
✚ C2 ✉ 32 Church Street ☎ 617/864 6100 ⏰ Lunch, dinner ⓜ Harvard Square

CASA ROMERO (££)
Romantic Back Bay eatery serving such rich dishes as chicken in a *mole poblano* (Poblano chilli) sauce. Eat alfresco in the courtyard.
✚ F5 ✉ 30 Gloucester Street ☎ 617/536 4341 ⏰ Dinner ⓜ Hynes/ICA

ASIAN & MIDDLE EASTERN

BOMBAY CLUB (££)
Buffet lunch is excellent
value in this stylish Indian
restaurant. Expect to pay
more for dinner.
✚ C3 ✉ 57 JFK Street,
Cambridge ☎ 617/661 8100
🕐 Lunch, dinner; Sun brunch
Ⓠ Harvard Square

CASABLANCA (£–££)
Next door to the Brattle
Theater, a favourite
hangout for film buffs,
Harvard folk and young
professionals. Check out
the murals in the bar from
the namesake film. Good
appetisers and Turkish-
Middle Eastern fare; also
good for vegetarians.
✚ C2 ✉ 40 Brattle Street
☎ 617/876 0999 🕐 Mon–
Fri lunch; daily dinner; Sat, Sun
brunch Ⓠ Harvard

**GRAND CHAU CHOW
& CHAU CHOW (£)**
Chinatown favourites on
opposite sides of the
street. Chau Chow is
pretty basic; Grand Chau
Chow, serving Hong Kong
style food, is classier.
✚ H5 ✉ 52 and 45 Beach
Street ☎ 617/426 6266,
617/292 5166 🕐 Lunch,
dinner. Daily till 2AM
Ⓠ Chinatown

GINZA (££)
'In' place for Japanese
food: superior sushi, *maki*
(sushi rolled in crisp
seaweed) and tempura.
✚ H5 ✉ 16 Hudson Street
☎ 617/338 2261 🕐 Lunch,
dinner. Tue–Sat till 4AM; Sun, Mon
till 2AM Ⓠ Chinatown

**JAE'S CAFÉ &
GRILL (££)**
Provides a Pan-Asian
menu – the speciality is

sushi. Also at 520
Columbus Avenue and
1281 Cambridge Street.
All very busy.
✚ G5 ✉ 212 Stuart Street
☎ 617/451 7788 🕐 Lunch,
dinner Ⓠ Boylston

MARY CHUNG (£)
Splendid Mandarin and
Szechuan-style food in an
unpromising Central
Square location.
✚ D4 ✉ 464 Massachusetts
Avenue, Cambridge ☎ 617/
864 1991 🕐 Wed–Mon lunch
and dinner Ⓠ Central Square

NEW SHANGHAI (£)
Somewhat more upmarket
than other Chinatown
eateries, specialises in
Shanghai-style cuisine. It's
developing a reputation as
a place Boston chefs go on
their days off. Unusual
cold appetisers (sautéed
aubergine with garlic
sauce, hot and sour
vegetables).
✚ H5 ✉ 21 Hudson Street
☎ 617/338 6688 🕐 Lunch,
dinner Ⓠ Chinatown

PHO PASTEUR (£)
Two small Vietnamese
eateries providing reliable
beef noodle soups and
other favourites.
✚ G5–H5 ✉ 682 Washington
Street; 8 Kneeland Street
☎ 617/482 7467, 617/451
0247 Ⓠ Chinatown

THAI VILLAGE (££)
Authentic Thai cuisine –
lemon grass shrimp soup
and mussel pancake –
shines in this elegant
South End restaurant.
✚ G6 ✉ 592 Tremont Street
☎ 617/536 6548 🕐 Mon–
Sat lunch; daily dinner
Ⓠ Back Bay

For vegetarians

Boston is becoming increasingly
vegetarian-friendly. More and
more restaurants include at least
one entrée, and many will make
up a vegetarian plate on request.
In Chinatown try Buddah's Delight
(✉ 3 Beach Street ☎ 617/
451 2395). Around the corner
from Symphony Hall, Cena,
pronounced 'Kay–na' (✉ 14a
Westland Avenue, off
Massachusetts Avenue ☎ 617/
262 1485). Downtown serves
sophisticated vegetarian fare as
well as fish dishes. Milk Street
Café (✉ 50 Milk Street
☎ 617/542 3663) is a
vegetarian-kosher luncheonette
that sells salads, soups and
vegetable sandwiches, plus
meatless entrées. Just off State
Street, Sultan's Kitchen (✉ 72
Broad Street ☎ 617/728
2828) is a Turkish/Middle Eastern
take-away (with a few tables);
good salads. Also try Border Café
(► 66); Casablanca, Chau Chow
and Jae's Café & Grill (see main
entries, this page).

BRUNCH, COFFEE, TEA & LATE EATING

Suggestions for children's meals

Bertucci's

Local pizza-pasta chain.

✉ 21 Brattle Street, Harvard Square, Cambridge

☎ 617/864 4748;

✉ Faneuil Hall

☎ 617/227 7889

Figs

Vast, gourmet pizzas and pastas.

✉ 42 Charles Street, Beacon Hill

☎ 617/742 3447;

✉ 67 Main Street, Charlestown

☎ 617/242 2229

Hard Rock Café

A (loud) family favourite.

✉ 131 Clarendon Street, near Hancock Tower

☎ 617/424 7625

Perennially popular is a *dim sum* lunch in Chinatown. Try Golden Palace (✉ 14 Tyler Street ☎ 617/423 4565) or Chau Chow City (✉ 83 Essex Street ☎ 617/338 8158). Skyline's Sunday brunch at the Museum of Science (☎ 617/723 2500) overlooks the Charles River and can be combined with a film in the IMAX cinema (brunch at 10 for a screening at noon, or brunch at noon, screening at 2).

BRUNCH

Weekend brunch is entrenched. Check out: Aujourd'hui, Chez Henri (► 62); Ritz Carlton, Sonsie (► 69); East Coast Grill (► 64); Henrietta's Table (► 66); Bombay Club (► 67); Skipjacks, Turner Fisheries (► 64); Museum of Science Skyline Brunch (► 34).

GARDNER MUSEUM CAFÉ (£)

Highly civilised weekend brunch, preferably before a (winter) afternoon concert.

➕ D6 ✉ 280 The Fenway ☎ 617/566 1088 🕐 Mon–Fri 11–4 🚇 Museum

HOUSE OF BLUES (££)

The Sunday Gospel Jazz Brunch at this Boston outpost of the LA-based chain is an institution. Eat from the phenomenal buffet at one long table to stirring Southern jazz and blues. Book ahead.

➕ C3 ✉ 96 Winthrop Street, Cambridge ☎ 617/491 2583 🕐 Seatings at 10, noon and 2

COFFEE

Branches of Au Bon Pain ('ABP') and Starbucks all over town. Otherwise, try:

BISCOTTIS PASTICCERIA

Favourite North End bakery with a mouth-watering window display.

➕ dII; H4 ✉ 95 Salem Street ☎ 617/227 8365 🚇 Haymarket

HI-RISE PIE COMPANY

Alfresco coffee and good pastries in Harvard Square's Blacksmith House. Built 1811, this was Henry W Longfellow's 'Village Blacksmith'.

➕ C2 ✉ 56 Brattle Street, Cambridge ☎ 617/492 3003 🚇 Harvard Square

REBECCA'S BAKERY & COFFEE

Home-made pastries, cake and fresh fruit tarts.

➕ aIV; G4 ✉ 70 Charles Street ☎ 617/742 9542 🚇 Charles/MGH

CAFFÈ PARADISO

Nice for an unhurried coffee or lunch in Harvard Square. Also in the North End (255 Hanover Street).

➕ C3 ✉ 1 Eliot Square ☎ 617/868 3240 🚇 Harvard Square

TO GO BAKERY

South End locals queue for the muffins, scones and cream cheese cake.

➕ F7 ✉ 314 Shawmut Avenue ☎ 617/482 1015 🕐 Mon–Fri from 6:30AM; Sat, Sun from 7 🚇 Back Bay

A SPECIAL TEA

THE BRISTOL (FOUR SEASONS HOTEL)

Traditional high tea daily at 3–4:30 (► 69 for details).

MUSEUM OF FINE ARTS

Tea and music in the Ladies' Committee Room.

➕ E6 ✉ 465 Huntington Avenue ☎ 617/267 9300 🕐 Tue–Fri 2:30–4 🚇 Museum

RITZ LOUNGE

Best behaviour for dainty sandwiches, English tea

cake, mini fruit tart.

✚ aV; G5 ✉ Ritz Carlton Hotel, 15 Arlington Street ☎ 617/536 5700 ◉ Daily 3–5:30 ⓠ Arlington

TEALUXE

Their motto is 'Over 140 teas and one coffee'. Few tables and a small selection of pastries, but plenty of tea choices.

✚ C3 ✉ Zero Brattle Street, Cambridge ☎ 617/441 0077 ◉ Mon–Sat 8AM–midnight; Sun 8AM–11PM ⓠ Harvard

LATE EATING

Bostonians generally eat early. For late eating, try Chinatown or:

THE BRISTOL (FOUR SEASONS HOTEL) (££)

Gorge on caloric desserts in the Viennese Dessert Buffet by the fire or overlooking the Public Garden. Also late dining.

✚ G5 ✉ 200 Boylston Street ☎ 617/338 4400 ◉ Sun–Thu 11–11; Fri, Sat 11AM–12:30AM. Viennese Dessert Buffet Fri, Sat (also seasonal Thu) 9PM–midnight ⓠ Arlington

CHEERS (BULL AND FINCH PUB) (£)

The place made famous by the popular TV series. Bar food served till late – wait until the tourists have departed.

✚ aIV; G5 ✉ 84 Beacon Street ☎ 617/227 9605 ◉ Daily 11AM–1:30AM ⓠ Arlington

FINALE (£)

Tucked behind the Four Seasons Hotel, serves light meals and elaborate desserts. Popular pre- and post-theatre. Try the $25 Chocolate Plate for Two.

✚ G5 ✉ 15 Columbus Avenue ☎ 617/423 3184 ◉ Mon–Fri lunch; dinner till midnight (Sun till 11, Mon till 10) ⓠ Arlington

MISTRAL (£££)

One of Boston's hippest dining rooms, a see-and-be-seen kind of place. Dramatic (but noisy) room, contemporary cuisine (grilled portobello mushroom 'carpaccio' with roasted peppers).

✚ G5 ✉ 223 Columbus Avenue ☎ 617/867 9300 ◉ Daily 5:30–midnight ⓠ Back Bay

MOON VILLA (£)

The food's not special – mainstream Chinese fare – but a late-night visit is an experience.

✚ H5 ✉ 19 Edinboro Street ☎ 617/423 2061 ◉ Daily till 4AM ⓠ Chinatown

SONSIE (££)

Hip haunt. Eclectic menu ranges from Vietnamese spring rolls to grilled vanilla-cured pork loin.

✚ F5 ✉ 327 Newbury Street ☎ 617/351 2500 ◉ Wed–Sat 7:30AM–midnight (rest of week till 11PM) ⓠ Hynes/ICA

SOUTH STREET DINER (£)

Classic hole-in-the-wall diner in the Leather District; eggs, burgers and coffee served at all hours.

✚ H5 ✉ 178 Kneeland Street ☎ 617/350 0028 ◉ 24 hours ⓠ South station

Also try: Top of the Hub (► 65); Border Café; Brew Moon (► 66); Casablanca (► 67).

Ice cream

Superb ice cream in Boston can found at Emack & Bolio (✉ 290 Newbury Street ☎ 617/247 8772), an ice cream, yogurt and juice bar, who claim to have invented the sublime cookies-and-cream ice cream. Billings & Stover Apothecary (✉ 41a Brattle Street, Harvard Square ☎ 617/547 0502) is an old-time 'drugstore' with a genuine soda fountain. Steve's and Herrell's premium ice creams are both named after local ice cream wizard Steve Herrell (✉ Faneuil Hall Marketplace ☎ 617/367 0569; ✉ 224 Newbury Street ☎ 617/236 0857 and at ✉ 15 Dunster Street, Harvard Square, Cambridge ☎ 617/ 497 2179). JP Licks is also on Newbury Street (✉ 617/236 1666) and Toscanini's has a branch in Harvard Square (✉ 1310 Massachusetts Avenue, Cambridge ☎ 617/ 491 5877).

DISTRICTS & DEPARTMENT STORES

There are several clearly defined shopping areas in Boston, each with its own personality. If you have time for only one spree, choose Newbury Street, which has to be one of the most beautiful streets for shoppers in the country.

NEWBURY STREET

Running west from the Public Garden to Massachusetts Avenue through the Back Bay, Newbury Street's Victorian houses make a colourful corridor of enticing shops, galleries and restaurants. Everything is here, from designer boutiques to second-hand clothes shops, from prestigious galleries to Tower Records, from names like Giorgio Armani to small independents, from pavement cafés to sophisticated restaurants. The east end of the street is the chic end, the west less so.

➕ F5 🔘 Arlington, Copley, Hynes/ICA

CHARLES STREET

This is another delightful street of shops and restaurants, running north from the Public Garden through the flat area of Beacon Hill. It specialises in antiques shops but has several nice gift shops and galleries too, and a selection of places where you can get a bite to eat.

➕ aIV; G4 🔘 Arlington, Charles

DOWNTOWN CROSSING

Street fashion and shoe shops, run-of-the-mill jewellery shops, camera shops and the like, plus the city's main department stores – and the legendary bargain hunters' mecca, Filene's Basement (➤ 72). Encompassing part of Washington Street, Winter Street and Bromfield Street, Downtown Crossing is mainly pedestrianised.

➕ cIV; H5 🔘 Downtown Crossing

FANEUIL HALL MARKETPLACE

Souvenirs and New England crafts keep company with worthwhile fashion, accessories, pewter, household-goods shops, a BosTix ticket agency booth (➤ 80), and plenty of eating options – all in and around three well-restored wharf buildings.

➕ aIII; H4 🔘 State

HARVARD SQUARE

Cambridge's Harvard Square is a maze of streets with dozens of bookshops (many stay open all evening), music shops and clothes shops – new and second-hand – much of it geared for the student population. It's an entertaining place too, with a wide variety of food and drink options. Check out Brattle Street, Church Street, Eliot Street (with the Charles Square complex just off), John F Kennedy Street and Dunster Street. As some of the chains have moved into the area, so some of the smaller local shops have moved or opened up, just north of Harvard, and there's now a clutch of

Sales tax

The 5 per cent sales tax does not apply to food or items of clothing under $175.

Opening times

Most shops are open until 6PM Monday to Saturday, sometimes later on Thursday and from 11 or noon to 6 on Sundays. In Harvard Square some shops stay open all evening.

Art galleries

Newbury Street is the place to go if you are interested in buying artwork – paintings, prints or sculpture. Many a pleasant hour can be spent browsing in the galleries here, stopping off in a café now and then. A concentration of them can be found between Arlington and Exeter streets and display works by 18th- and 19th-century in addition to contemporary artists.

70

funky clothes and gift shops on Massachusetts Avenue heading towards Porter Square.

✚ C2–C3 ⓜ Harvard Square

PRUDENTIAL CENTER AND COPLEY PLACE

A vast undercover complex in the Back Bay that encompasses two malls (see below), several hotels and the Hynes Convention Center.

MALLS

CAMBRIDGESIDE GALLERIA

Scores of shops on three levels, some of which will appeal to the younger generation. Fashion outlets include Banana Republic, The Limited, J. Crew, Original Levi's Store and Talbots. There are several footwear places (such as Nine West and Overland), music shops, a Disney shop, barrows, eateries, branches of department stores Filene's and Sears.

✚ F3 ✉ 100 Cambridgeside Place ⓣ Mon–Sat 10–9:30; Sun 11–7 ⓜ Lechmere or Kendall Square; free shuttle bus

CHESTNUT HILL

Mall at Chestnut Hill for stylish shopping in a classy suburb.

✚ Off map at A7 ✉ Hammond Pond Parkway, Chestnut Hill ⓜ Chestnut Hill and 15 minute walk

COPLEY PLACE

Copley is more refined than 'the Pru' (the Prudential Center), to which it is connected by a covered bridge over Huntington Avenue.

Elegant shops such as Tiffany's and Neiman-Marcus jostle with national chains and outlets for trendy kitchenware, high-tech gadgets and very good crafts. There is a cinema complex.

✚ F6 ✉ Huntington Avenue ⓣ Mon–Sat 10–7; Sun noon–6 ⓜ Copley

PRUDENTIAL CENTER

A dozen clothes shops (including Ann Taylor, Chico's, Claiborne Men, Structure and Original Levi's), some shoe and accessories shops, gift and speciality (such as stationery) shops and a hardware shop. Also home to department stores Saks Fifth Avenue and Lord & Taylor, a post office, cashpoints, Movenpick's superb food courts and Legal Sea Foods.

✚ F5–F6 ✉ Between Boylston Street and Huntington Avenue ⓣ Mon–Sat 10–8; Sun 11–6 ⓜ Prudential

DEPARTMENT STORES

Boston's two major department stores face each other in Downtown Crossing: Macy's, the bigger and Filene's. Underneath Filene's is Filene's Basement (➤ 72). Other shops have branches in malls (see above). In Harvard Square there is The Coop, or the Harvard Cooperative Society. Strong on books and posters, it was started as a non-profit shop for students in 1882 and is now the biggest department store in the centre of Cambridge.

Outlet shopping

Factory outlet shopping is now one of New England's biggest draws for visitors. The major outlet centres are out of Boston, but not more than an hour away. A whole range of merchandise – clothes, shoes, household and electrical goods, luggage – is discounted, sometimes as much as 70 per cent off the normal retail price. All the well-known brand names keep cropping up, including Levi's, Calvin Klein, Liz Claiborne, Van Heusen, Ralph Lauren, Donna Karan, Bally, Timberland, Tommy Hilfiger and Eddie Bauer.

Closest to Boston are:

Worcester Common

More than 90 well-known designer and manufacturer's shops and about one hour west by Peter Pan bus from South station (daily 9AM, returning 4PM) or by car on Route 1/90.

Fall River

Particularly known for linen, kitchenware and furniture. One hour south of Boston.

Kittery

In Maine has more than 100 shops and is about an hour north on Route 95.

Freeport

Also in Maine, north of Kittery – the birthplace of outlet shopping, and home of outdoor clothing specialist L L Bean.

CLOTHES

Clothes for sport and the outdoor life

More casual clothes will be found in some of the shops listed under Shoes, Outdoor Clothes & Sports Equipment (➤ 74).

Levi's

Visitors from abroad often want to buy Levi's jeans, which are sold here at prices way below those at home. Because so many jeans were being bought up in the States, shipped home and sold at a profit, Levi's have limited the number of jeans bought in one lot to six. Original Levi's Stores (Pru Center, CambridgeSide Galleria and 33 Summer Street) have an extensive range but are not the cheapest place to buy. One of the cheaper places to find a good range is the Mass Army & Navy.

➕ C3 ✉ Massachusetts Avenue, Harvard Square 🚇 Harvard Square

ALAN BILZERIAN

A fun one for window shopping (or buying, of course, if you're very rich or very outrageous) for little numbers from Jean-Paul Gaultier, Katharine Hamnett and the like.

➕ G5 ✉ 34 Newbury Street ☎ 617/536 1001 🚇 Arlington

BETSEY JOHNSON

Pretty things in natural fabrics and locally knitted sweaters.

➕ F5 ✉ 201 Newbury Street ☎ 617/236 7072 🚇 Copley

CHICO'S

Comfortable, casual but stylish and affordable women's clothes, just that little bit different. Skirts, trousers, waistcoats, and tops in natural fibres.

➕ F6 ✉ Prudential Center ☎ 617/247 3771 🚇 Prudential

CLOTHWARE

Contemporary women's clothing, lots of knits and linen. Nice lingerie. Wacky hats.

➕ C2 ✉ 52 Brattle Street ☎ 617/261 6441 🚇 Harvard

DEBORAH MANN ATELIER

Deborah Mann creates sophisticated but comfortable dresses, trousers, skirts and tops in minimalist, Japanese-inspired style. This small shop carries her designs and similar clothes by other designers. Moderate prices.

➕ C1 ✉ 1691 Massachusetts Avenue ☎ 617/576 0123 🚇 Harvard, then walk or bus 77

EILEEN FISHER

Natural fabrics in elegant, simple designs for women's smart, casual day and evening wear. Rich colour range.

➕ F6 ✉ Copley Place ☎ 617/536 6800 🚇 Copley

EMPORIO ARMANI

Slightly less haute couture but more accessible price-wise than Giorgio Armani (No. 22 Newbury Street). Popular café (on the pavement in summer).

➕ G5 ✉ 210 Newbury Street ☎ 617/262 7300 🚇 Copley

FILENE'S BASEMENT

A Boston institution, this is the original bargain basement, beneath Filene's department store but separately managed. When a manufacturer or shop has overstock (or goes under) the goods end up here and are sold off at vastly discounted prices. The price is then marked down again and again until sold. The Basement gets incredibly crowded, so avoid lunchtime and weekends.

➕ cIV; H5 ✉ Washington Street at Summer Street ☎ 617/642 2011 🚇 Downtown Crossing

GREGZ

Funky casual wear for men. Big shirts – think bowling league chic – and loose trousers.

➕ C1 ✉ 1766 Massachusetts Avenue ☎ 617/441 89890 🚇 Porter

JASMINE/SOLA/ SOLA MEN

Chic young designer clothes and shoes in

Harvard Square but that's too expensive for the average student.

🕂 C2 ✉ 37 Brattle Street
☎ 617/354 6043
🚇 Harvard

LOUIS, BOSTON

High quality, expensive clothing for men and women in a spacious shop just off Newbury Street. Nice café.

🕂 G5 ✉ 234 Berkeley Street
☎ 617/262 6100
🚇 Arlington

PAVO REAL

Cotton, silk and wool knitwear in rich (and subtle) colours and patterns. In Copley Place.

🕂 F5 ✉ 100 Huntingdon Avenue ☎ 617/437 6699
🚇 Copley

PEPPERWEED

Upmarket women's boutique. Good choice for special occasion or creative professional dressing. Helpful staff will match you with that perfect dress.

🕂 C1 ✉ 1684 Massachusetts Avenue ☎ 617/547 7561
🚇 Harvard, then walk or bus 77

RICCARDI

Dolce & Gabbana and other pricey Euro-chic labels for the young and the trendy.

🕂 F5 ✉ 116 Newbury Street
☎ 617/266 3158 🚇 Copley

SERENDIPITY

Hip choice of ethnic designs from India, South America and Africa.

🕂 C3 ✉ 1312 Massachusetts Avenue and 229 Newbury Steet
☎ 617/661 7143
🚇 Harvard

SIMON'S

Impeccable men's tailoring at this classic Proper Bostonian shop in Copley Square. Alterations done on the premises.

🕂 F5 ✉ 220 Clarendon Street
☎ 617/266 2345 🚇 Copley

TALBOTS

Classic women's clothes for work or leisure. Neat suits, shirts, trousers, coats, casual wear and night wear. Full range of petite sizes.

🕂 F5 ✉ 500 Boylston Street and 25 School Street ☎ 617/262 2981 🚇 Arlington, Copley

URBAN OUTFITTERS

Where the young come to get that rugged look. Funky household goods.

🕂 C3 ✉ 11 JFK Street/Brattle Street and 321 Newbury Street
☎ 617/864 0070
🚇 Harvard

VICTORIA'S SECRET

The ultimate in silk, satin and lace. Also in the malls.

🕂 dIII; H4 ✉ Faneuil Hall Marketplace and in malls
☎ 617/248 9761 🚇 State, Government Center

SECOND-HAND DESIGN

For that designer label you can't afford at a Newbury Street boutique.

THE CLOSET

Men and women's fashion.

🕂 F5 ✉ 175 Newbury Street
☎ 617/536 1919 🚇 Copley

SECOND TIME AROUND

For women only. Also at 8 Eliot Street, Cambridge.

🕂 F5 ✉ 167 Newbury Street
☎ 617/247 3504 🚇 Copley

Children's clothes

Calliope

For infants and young children. Largest selection of stuffed animals in Harvard Square; also baby toys.

✉ 33 Brattle Street
☎ 617/876 4149

Baby Gap/Gap Kids

Popular chain. Also in Copley Place, and at 15 Brattle Street, Harvard Square in Cambridge

✉ 201 Newbury Street
☎ 617/424 8778

The Red Wagon

Brightly coloured, creatively casual T-shirt sets, dresses and more for babies and young children. Cool kids' jewellery, too.

✉ 49 Charles Street
☎ 617/524 9402

Saturday's Child

Swank special-occasion (and expensive) outfits for infants, preschoolers and kids. Many from European designers.

✉ 1762 Massachusetts Avenue
☎ 617/661 6402

Talbots Kids

Kids' branch of classic women's shop (in the Prudential Center). Traditionally styled casual wear.

✉ 800 Boylston Street
☎ 617/266 9400

73

SHOES & OUTDOOR GEAR

More choice

These large outdoor activity shops are a little way out of the centre, all on Commonwealth Avenue.

Eastern Mountain Sports

Hiking, backpacking, camping, mountaineering, cross-country skiing.

✉ 1041 Commonwealth Avenue
☎ 617/254 4250

Ski Market

Skiing, snowboarding, in-line skating, biking. Ski and snowboard hire. Good children's section.

✉ 860 Commonwealth Avenue
☎ 617/731 6100

Wayland Golf Shop

Best names in clubs, bags, shoes and more.

✉ 890 Commonwealth Avenue
☎ 617/277 3999

For bike hire, try Back Bay Bicycles (✉ 336 Newbury Street ☎ 617/247 2336) and check out Blades (see main entry on this page) if you want to hire in-line skates and skateboards, or even have lessons; helpful staff.

SHOES

ALLEN EDMONDS

Top quality shoes in classic styles come in all widths, sizes 5–18.
✚ G5 ✉ 36 Newbury Street
☎ 617/247 3363
Ⓜ Arlington

FOOTPATHS

Elegant shoes for men and women, plus a full range of hiking boots.
✚ clV; H5 ✉ 489 Washington Street ☎ 617/338 6008
Ⓜ Downtown Crossing

NIKETOWN

Large, state-of-the-art shop, arranged by pavilion: men's and women's training and running, golf, basketball, football, tennis and more.
✚ F5 ✉ 200 Newbury Street
☎ 617/267 3400 Ⓜ Copley

OVERLAND TRADING

The wide selection of hiking shoes, boots and sneakers here includes Timberland, Sebago. Also in CambridgeSide Galleria.
✚ F5 ✉ 176 Newbury Street
☎ 617/424 7615 Ⓜ Copley

THE ROCKPORT STORE

The main outlet here for Rockport shoes and boots. Also at 83 Newbury Street. Stop by for a free bottle of water or a foot massage while you're checking out the shoes.
✚ dlI; H4 ✉ Faneuil Hall Marketplace ☎ 617/367 9996 Ⓜ State, Government Center

THE TANNERY

Wide range of hiking boots and sneakers (Vans, Timberland, Sebago, Rockport). Also in Brattle Street, Harvard Square.
✚ G5 ✉ 400 Boylston Street
☎ 617/267 0899
Ⓜ Arlington

OUTDOOR GEAR

BLADES

Good selection of board and skate gear. Also at 38 JFK Street, Harvard Square in Cambridge. Both do rentals and lessons. Smaller branch at 22 Newbury Street.
✚ F5 ✉ 349a Newbury Street
☎ 617/437 6300
Ⓜ Hynes/ICA

DAKINI

Everything fleece for men, women and children. Fleece boxer shorts, anyone? Designed more for urban style than rugged outdoor wear. Between Harvard and Porter squares.
✚ C1 ✉ 1704 Massachusetts Avenue ☎ 617/864 7661
Ⓜ Harvard, then walk or bus 77

HILTON'S TENT CITY

Good place for hiking and camping.
✚ dlI; H4 ✉ 272 Friend Street
☎ 617/227 9104 Ⓜ North station

WILDERNESS HOUSE

All the latest for hiking, camping, tennis, swimming, fishing and roller blading. Also at 1048 Commonwealth Avenue (opposite Eastern Mountain Sports – see panel).
✚ clV; H5 ✉ 9 Spring Lane, off Washington Street
☎ 617/426 4440 Ⓜ State

Books, Maps & Music

BOOKS & MAPS

Cambridge, and Harvard Square in particular, has an amazing concentration of independent bookshops; just a handful are mentioned here. Pick up a complete guide from the information kiosk by Harvard Square T. Chainstores such as Borders and Barnes & Noble are to be found throughout Boston and Cambridge.

AVENUE VICTOR HUGO

An institution. Huge collection of second-hand books on every subject.
✚ E5　✉ 339 Newbury Street
☎ 617/266 7746
🚇 Hynes/ICA

BRATTLE BOOKSTORE

A treasure trove of rare and second-hand books with a good section on Boston and New England.
✚ bIV; G5　✉ 9 West Street
☎ 617/542 0210　🚇 Park

GLOBE CORNER BOOKSTORE

Great for travel books and maps. Also at 28 Church Street, Cambridge.
✚ F5　✉ 500 Boylston Street
☎ 617/859 8008　🚇 Copley

GROLIER POETRY BOOKSHOP

The US's only shop devoted entirely to poetry.
✚ C3　✉ 6 Plympton Street, Cambridge　☎ 617/547 4648
🚇 Harvard

HARVARD BOOKSTORE

Venerable favourite for academic titles and other kinds of non-fiction books.
✚ C3　✉ 1256 Massachusetts Avenue, Cambridge　☎ 617/661 1515　🚇 Harvard

RAND MCNALLY MAP & TRAVEL

Good range of maps and guides to New England – and elsewhere, too.
✚ dIII; H4　✉ 84 State Street
☎ 617/720 1125　🚇 State

WORDSWORTH

An absolute warren. Discounted prices.
✚ C3　✉ 30 Brattle Street
☎ 617/354 5201　🚇 Harvard

MUSIC

CHEAPO RECORDS

Used rock, blues, jazz albums, LPs and 45s.
✚ D4　✉ 645 Massachusetts Avenue, Cambridge　☎ 617/354 4455　🚇 Central

HMV

Huge. Covers all tastes in music.
✚ C3　✉ 1 Brattle Square, Cambridge　☎ 617/868 9696
🚇 Harvard

NEWBURY COMICS

The hippest record shop in town. Pop CDs plus T-shirts, posters and comics.
✚ E5　✉ 332 Newbury Street and 36 JFK Street, Cambridge
☎ 617/236 4930
🚇 Hynes/ICA

TOWER RECORDS

The largest Tower shop in the world. There's another in Cambridge at 95 Mount Auburn Street.
✚ E5　✉ 360 Newbury Street
☎ 617/247 5900
🚇 Hynes/ICA

Shopping with/for children

In Harvard Square:

Curious George goes to WordsWorth

WordsWorth's children's book shop, full of delights.
✉ Brattle Street　☎ 617/498 0062

Harvard Coop

It's a peaceful oasis of children's books hidden in the shop's basement. A calm, quiet place to browse – with or without the kids.
✉ 1400 Massachusetts Avenue
☎ 617/499 2000

Learningsmith

Superb choice of books, games and educational toys for children of all ages.
✉ 25 Brattle Street
☎ 617/661 6008

In Faneuil Hall Marketplace, Kites of Boston is a good bet and in Back Bay there is the toy emporium FAO Schwarz (✉ 440 Boylston Street ☎ 617/262 5900)

Museums with particularly good shops for children are:
the Children's Museum (➤ 59), the Museum of Fine Arts (➤ 28), the Museum of Science (➤ 34).

CRAFTS, GIFTS & HOUSEHOLD GOODS

Antiques

Cambridge Antique Market
150 dealers selling china, glass, quilts, clothes, silver, jewellery and collectables; across the river; café.
✉ 201 Monsignor O'Brien Highway
☎ 617/868 9655
Ⓒ Closed Mon

Charles Street
Pretty street at the foot of Beacon Hill lined with a string of 30 or so antique shops (mostly fairly expensive) – in basements, on first floors and down alleys; and there are a few more in River Street. Between them, you'll find everything from 18th- and 19th-century European furniture to porcelain, lighting, linen and garden furnishings.
Ⓜ Arlington, Charles

Minot Hall Antique Center
200 dealers in a restored 1859 building in the South End. Furniture, paintings, American decorative arts, silver and more.
✉ Washington Avenue (off Massachusetts Avenue)
☎ 617/236 7800
Ⓒ Closed Mon

CRAFTS

ALIANZA
High-calibre contemporary crafts: jewellery, glass, fantastic teapots. Gift vouchers.
✚ F5 ✉ 154 Newbury Street
☎ 617/262 2385 Ⓜ Copley

ARTFUL HAND
Contemporary American crafts of exceptional quality: woven silk scarfs, woodwork, ceramics, glass. In Copley Place mall.
✚ F6 ✉ 36 Copley Place
☎ 617/262 9601 Ⓜ Copley, Prudential

BEADWORKS
Vast array of beads for make-it-yourself jewellery. Also in Cambridge at 23 Church Street, Harvard Square.
✚ E5 ✉ 349 Newbury Street
☎ 617/247 7227
Ⓜ Hynes/ICA

CAMBRIDGE ARTISTS' COOPERATIVE
Quilts, weaving, jewellery, scarves, bowls – all made locally and mostly affordable.
✚ C2 ✉ 59a Church Street
☎ 617/868 4434
Ⓜ Harvard

SIGNATURE
Top American crafts in wood, glass, ceramic and woven fabrics. On the fringe of Faneuil.
✚ dIII; H4 ✉ 24 North Street
☎ 617/227 4885 Ⓜ State, Government Center

SOCIETY OF ARTS AND CRAFTS
Contemporary ceramics, glass, woodwork, jewellery of the highest quality.

✚ F5 ✉ 175 Newbury Street
☎ 617/266 1810 Ⓜ Copley

GIFTS & HOUSEHOLD GOODS

For art see panel (► 70)

BLACK INK
An eclectic selection of funky gifts and novelties: shark staplers, alphabet cookie cutters, bright green frog banks, architectural city guides.
✚ aIII; G4 ✉ 101 Charles Street ☎ 617/723 3883
Ⓜ Charles

BROMFIELD PEN SHOP
Pens, from vintage early 1900s models, to new Montblanc, Cross; and cheap disposables.
✚ cIV; H5 ✉ 5 Bromfield Street ☎ 617/482 9053
Ⓜ Park

BROOKSTONE
Hundreds of nifty little gadgets.
✚ F6 ✉ Copley Place
☎ 617/267 4308 Ⓜ Copley

CRATE & BARREL
Well-designed, affordable household goods: Egyptian cotton sheets, table linen, hand-blown glass, kitchen utensils.
✚ dIII; H4 ✉ Faneuil Hall Marketplace and in Copley Place Mall ☎ 617/742 6025
Ⓜ State, Governement Center

EUGENE GALLERIES
A shop specialising in old maps and prints, with a good selection covering Boston and New England.
✚ aIV; G4 ✉ 76 Charles Street ☎ 617/227 3062
Ⓜ Charles

FRESH EGGS

'Everything for your nest' – or almost everything – in the South End. Candles, linen, sparkling pots and pans.

✚ G6 ✉ 58 Clarendon Street at Chandler Street ☎ 617/227 4646 ⚇ Back Bay

J OLIVER'S

Crammed with tasteful and fun gifts.

✚ aIV; G4 ✉ 38 Charles Street ☎ 617/723 3388 ⚇ Charles

LINENS ON THE HILL

Fine French linen – sheets, pillowcases, tablecloths. Also nightgowns and robes.

✚ aIV; G4 ✉ 52 Charles Street ☎ 617/227 1255 ⚇ Charles

LOULOU'S LOST & FOUND

If it might have been on a 1920s ocean liner, Loulou's has it – dishes, tea service, silver-plated utensils and other gift ideas.

✚ F5 ✉ 121 Newbury Street ☎ 617/859 8593 ⚇ Copley

MDF

Modern Designer Furnishings: finely crafted contemporary picture frames, vases, serving pieces, lamps and small tables. In Harvard Square.

✚ C3 ✉ 19 Brattle Street ☎ 617/491 2789 ⚇ Harvard

MATSU

Chic gifts and (a few) clothes, many oriental, including the Muji range of stationery goods.

✚ F5 ✉ 259 Newbury Street

☎ 617/266 9707 ⚇ Copley, Hynes/ICA

NOSTALGIA FACTORY

Thousands of original film posters (some vintage), old signs, advertisements and more. In the North End.

✚ dII; H4 ✉ 51 North Margin Street (off Salem Street) ⚇ Haymarket

RUGG ROAD PAPER

Handmade papers by the roll or sheet; paste papers, woodblocks, inks, ribbons, sealing wax, handbound albums and notebooks. Books (and classes) on papermaking and book binding.

✚ aIII; G5 ✉ 105 Charles Street ☎ 617/742 0002 ⚇ Charles

SEASONINGS

Traditional cookware, French table linen, brushes of all sorts, kitchen utensils. Bridal registry.

✚ aIII; G5 ✉ 113 Beacon Street ☎ 617/227 2810 ⚇ Charles

STODDARD'S

Tiny shop packed to the gills with every conceivable type of knife and scissor. Irresistible.

✚ F6 ✉ Copley Place ☎ 617/536 8688 ⚇ Copley

WILLIAMS-SONOMA

For the cook who has everything – or so you thought till you came in here: from Dualit toasters and heart-shaped muffin baking trays to French table linen and flour sack towels. In Copley Place.

✚ F6 ✉ Copley Place ☎ 617/262 5892 ⚇ Copley

Food

For New England specialities, wine, beers and gourmet foods try: Cardullo's in Harvard Square (✉ 6 Brattle Street ☎ 617/491 8888). Explore the delis and *pasticcerias* of the Italian North End. Real food lovers can join a three-hour North End Market Tour, with specialist Michele Topor (☎ 617/523 6032 ⚇ Wed; Sat 10AM, 2PM). For fruit and vegetables there's Boston's only street market, Blackstone Market – known as the 'Haymarket', – near Faneuil Hall Marketplace (✉ Blackstone Street ⚇ Fridays and Saturdays only). Convenient if you're shopping in the Pru is Marché Movenpick, a grocer's shop within the mall (✉ Prudential Center, Huntingdon Avenue entrance). Pick up gourmet picnic foods from Savenor's (✉ 160 Charles Street ☎ 617/723 6328) – cheeses, patés, breads, fruits. Also the place to shop if you're looking for venison, lion steak, zebra and other exotic meats.

CLASSICAL MUSIC, OPERA & DANCE

Star of the classical music scene is the Boston Symphony Orchestra, which performs at Symphony Hall (below). Also worth considering are the many high-calibre, free performances such as those by the Boston Pops Orchestra (see Hatch Memorial Shell below).

Choral and early music groups

Boston has more than its fair share of choirs and early music groups, including the oldest music organisation in the US, the Handel & Haydn Society (☎ 617/266 3605) – established in 1815 and still performing regularly at Symphony Hall and Jordan Hall. Other groups to look for are Boston Camerata (☎ 617/262 2092), for medieval music; Chorus Pro Musica (☎ 617/267 7442), for choral music from the Renaissance to the present; and the Cantata Singers (☎ 617/267 6502) – based at Jordan Hall – for Bach to contemporary works.

CONCERT HALLS

BERKLEE PERFORMANCE CENTER

This Back Bay venue seats 1,220 and hosts varied concerts by international performers and by the students and staff of the Berklee College of Music.
➕ E6 ✉ 136 Massachusetts Avenue ☎ 617/266 7455, 617/747 2261 Ⓜ Hynes Convention Center

BOSTON UNIVERSITY CONCERT HALL

Students show off their musical talents, in free public concerts.
➕ D5 ✉ Tsai Performance Center, 685 Commonwealth Avenue ☎ 617/353 6467 Ⓜ Boston University East

HATCH MEMORIAL SHELL

The Boston Pops Orchestra gives free evening concerts at this site on the Charles River Esplanade throughout July. The highlight is the 4th of July concert, with fireworks. Locals come with a picnic.
➕ G4 ✉ Esplanade, Embankment Road ☎ 617/ 727 0627 Ⓜ Charles, Arlington

JORDAN HALL

This glittering and acoustically perfect venue in the prestigious New England Conservatory showcases the resident Boston Philharmonic, Boston Baroque, Cantata Singers and Boston Gay Men's Chorus. Conservatory students perform free concerts year round.
➕ F6 ✉ 30 Gainsborough Street, one block west of Symphony Hall ☎ 617/536 2412 Ⓜ Symphony

SANDERS THEATRE

A 1,200-seat neo-Gothic theatre at Harvard, with a varied programme of classical music and other fare.
➕ C2 ✉ Quincy Street at Cambridge Street, Cambridge ☎ 617/496 2222 Ⓜ Harvard Square

SYMPHONY HALL

'Symphony' is home of the world-renowned Boston Symphony Orchestra for seven months of the year. From October to April the orchestra performs on Friday afternoons, Saturday, Tuesday and Thursday evenings. Open rehearsals are held some Wednesday evenings and Thursday mornings. The Boston Pops Orchestra concerts (started in 1885 and still as popular as ever) are held in May and June before moving to the Hatch Memorial Shell (see above) in July.
➕ F6 ✉ 301 Massachusetts Avenue ☎ 617/266 1200, 617/266 1492 Ⓜ Symphony

SMALLER VENUES & CHAMBER MUSIC

EMMANUEL CHURCH

A Bach cantata every Sunday (September to May).

➕ G9 ✉ 15 Newbury Street
☎ 617/536 3355
🚇 Arlington

ISABELLA STEWART GARDNER MUSEUM

The great patron of arts and music began hosting chamber concerts in the Tapestry Room of her Venetian-style mansion (► 27), and the museum still runs concerts here on weekends (September to May).

➕ G5 ✉ 280 The Fenway
☎ 617/566 1401
🚇 Museum

KING'S CHAPEL

Free concerts Tuesdays (12:15); vocal and organ recitals.

➕ D6 ✉ 58 Tremont Street
☎ 617/523 1749 🚇 Park, Government Center

MUSEUM OF FINE ARTS

Baroque chamber concerts by the Boston Museum Trio and others, in the Remis Auditorium on Sunday afternoons (September to May), jazz concerts in the courtyard on Wednesday evenings in summer (► 28).

➕ E6 ✉ 465 Huntington Avenue ☎ 617/267 9300
🚇 Museum

TRINITY CHURCH

This architectural landmark (► 32) makes a wonderful backdrop for free organ and choir recitals, Fridays (12:15).

➕ F5 ✉ Copley Square
☎ 617/536 0944 🚇 Copley

OPERA & DANCE

BALLET THEATER OF BOSTON AND BOSTON BALLET

See Emerson Majestic and the Wang Center below.

BOSTON LYRIC OPERA

A fast-growing opera company that performs several productions a season at the Shubert Theater (► 81).

✉ 45 Franklin Street (company offices) ☎ 617/542 6772

DANCE UMBRELLA

Programmes an exciting season of contemporary dance, ranging from local hip-hop groups to avant-garde international performers.

➕ D4 ✉ 515 Washington Street (company offices)
☎ 617/482 7570

EMERSON MAJESTIC THEATER

Innovative performances by the Ballet Theater of Boston (☎ 617/262 0961), and by visiting troupes who explore other dance forms, such as flamenco.

➕ G5 ✉ 219 Tremont Street
☎ 617/824 8000
🚇 Boylston

WANG CENTER FOR PERFORMING ARTS

A 1920s movie palace used for concerts, opera, dance and the impressive Boston Ballet (☎ 617/695 6950), which performs classical and modern dance.

➕ G5 ✉ 270 Tremont Street
☎ 617/482 9393
🚇 Boylston

Alternative dance

Contemporary and ethnic dance troupes perform at venues all over the city and beyond. In Boston, these include the Dance Collective and Art of Black Dance and Music (☎ 617/666 1859). In Cambridge, look for the Multicultural Arts Center (✉ 41 2nd Street ☎ 617/577 1400), and the Dance Complex (✉ 536 Massachusetts Avenue ☎ 617/547 9363). In spring, a series of performances and workshops is held every year by the 30-member Mandala Folk Dance Ensemble (☎ 617/868 3641).

79

Theatre & Cinema

Tickets

BosTix sell half-price theatre tickets on the day of the show (from 11AM). As a full-fledged Ticketmaster outlet, it also sells full-price tickets in advance for venues in Boston and the rest of New England. Booths are at:

✉ Faneuil Hall Marketplace
🕐 Tue–Sat 10–6; Sun 11–4;
✉ Copley Square
🕐 Mon–Sat 10–6; Sun 11–4;
✉ Holyoke Center in Harvard Square
🕐 Mon–Sat 10–6; Sun 11–4.
Tickets cover theatre, concerts, museums, sports events and trolley tours. All are sold for cash only.

Boston, once regarded as something of a theatrical backwater, has now a proliferation of fringe, student and innovative companies, adding spice to the worthy mainstream fare. There is also a wide choice of cinemas showing alternative films.

THEATRE

AMERICAN REPERTORY THEATER

A highly regarded professional repertory company based in Harvard Square and staging a wide range of classical and original drama.
➕ C4 ✉ Loeb Drama Center, 64 Brattle Street, Cambridge ☎ 617/547 8300 🚇 Harvard Square

BOSTON CENTER FOR THE ARTS

Four stages provide the space for several contemporary theatre companies, including the resident Coyote Theater, bringing new life to Boston's theatrical scene.
➕ G6 ✉ 539 Tremont Street ☎ 617/426 7700 🚇 Back Bay

CHARLES PLAYHOUSE

Shear Madness is a comedy whodunnit set in a hairdresser's, which has played here since 1980.
➕ G5 ✉ 74 Warrenton Street ☎ 617/426 5225 🚇 Boylston

COLONIAL THEATER

This lush, beautifully restored, turn-of-the-century theatre stages pre-Broadway productions as well as concerts, and other performing arts events.
➕ G5 ✉ 106 Boylston Street ☎ 617/426 9366 🚇 Boylston

EMERSON MAJESTIC THEATER (▶ 79)

HASTY PUDDING THEATER

Home to the touring Harvard's Hasty Pudding Theatricals company and to the American Repertory Theater's annual 'New Stages' series of contemporary plays.
➕ C3 ✉ 12 Holyoke Street, Cambridge ☎ 617/495 5205 🚇 Harvard Square

HUNTINGTON THEATER COMPANY

From Boston University's resident professional troupe; includes European and American, classical and modern, comedies and musicals.
➕ F6 ✉ 264 Huntington Avenue ☎ 617/266 0800 🚇 Symphony

LYRIC STAGE

Classics and new American shows are the speciality of this venue on the second floor of the YWCA building.
➕ F5 ✉ 140 Clarendon Street ☎ 617/437 7172 🚇 Back Bay

PUPPET SHOWPLACE THEATER

The trip out to suburban Brookline is well worth while for children – and adults – who enjoy puppetry.
➕ C7 ✉ 32 Station Street, Brookline ☎ 617/731 6400 🕐 Performances year round;

call for times 🔊 Brookline Village (green line D)

SHUBERT THEATER

An institution, founded in 1910, in the heart of the Theater District, which produces major pre- and post-Broadway shows.
✚ G5 ✉ 265 Tremont Street ☎ 617/482 9393
🔊 Boylston

WILBUR THEATER

A small theatre offering new and classic drama.
✚ G5 ✉ 246 Tremont Street ☎ 617/423 4008
🔊 Boylston

CINEMAS

BOSTON PUBLIC LIBRARY

The occasional film series usually features lesser-known old films.
✚ F5 ✉ Copley Square ☎ 617/536 5400 🔊 Copley

BRATTLE THEATER

Old films and film festivals attract connoisseurs to this small, one-screen cinema.
✚ C3 ✉ 40 Brattle Street, Cambridge ☎ 617/876 6837
🔊 Harvard Square

COOLIDGE CORNER THEATER

A fine art deco Brookline venue showing an interesting and intelligent selection of vintage and contemporary films.
✚ C6 ✉ 290 Harvard Street, Brookline ☎ 617/734 2501
🔊 Coolidge Corner (green line C)

HARVARD FILM ARCHIVE

Several daily showings of cult and independent films at Harvard's Carpenter Center for the Visual Arts.
✚ C3 ✉ 24 Quincy Street, Cambridge ☎ 617/495 4700
🔊 Harvard Square

LANDMARK'S KENDALL SQUARE CINEMA

A multi-screen cinema also showing offbeat and foreign films. (There's a free shuttle bus every 20 minutes from Kendall station to CambridgeSide Galleria to the cinema.)
✚ F4 ✉ 1 Kendall Square, Cambridge ☎ 617/494 9800
🔊 Kendall, then walk or shuttle bus

MUSEUM OF FINE ARTS

International, early films, local interest and other offbeat films at the Remis Auditorium (▶ 28).
✚ E6 ✉ 465 Huntington Avenue ☎ 617/267 9300
🔊 Museum

SONY/LOEWS THEATERS

The Nickelodeon, near Boston University, and Harvard Square Theater are commercial multi-screen cinemas that also show independent and foreign films. The central Copley Place Theater, a commercial multiplex, shows first-runs.
✚ D5 ✉ 606 Commonwealth Avenue ☎ 617/424 1500
🔊 Kenmore, Blanford Street (green line B)
✚ C2 ✉ 10 Church Street, Cambridge ☎ 617/864 4580
🔊 Harvard
✚ F6 ✉ Copley Place ☎ 617/266 1300 🔊 Copley

A bit of variety

Fans of old-time vaudeville might like to take a trip out of Boston to Beverly, where Le Grand David and His Own Spectacular Magic Company offer good old-fashioned entertainment at:

Cabot Street Cinema Theater ✉ 286 Cabot Street 🕐 Sun; some Sats; hols

Larcom Theater ✉ 13 Wallis Street ☎ 978/927 3677

CLUBS & BARS

Waterfront concerts

Summer pop concerts are held in the BankBoston Pavilion on Fan Pier (✉ 290 Northern Avenue ☎ 617/374 9000, 617/737 6100). Tickets are expensive, but with the views of the downtown skyline, you may not mind.

Quieter choices

If you'd rather hear yourself think than groove the night away, check out Boston hotels' lounge bars — many with low-key music, some with food. Try the Oak Bar, in the glittering Fairmount Copley Plaza Hotel, Copley Square (► 84); Turner Fisheries Bar at Westin Hotel, Huntington Avenue, where a jazz trio (generally) plays Thursdays through Sundays; the Bristol Lounge in the Four Seasons Hotel (► 69), where classical piano or jazz music accompanies the sublime Viennese Dessert Buffet; the Atrium Lounge at the Regal Bostonian Hotel, Faneuil Hall, where a jazz trio performs in the Atrium Lounge Friday and Saturday evenings. See also the Regattabar and Scullers entries.

JAZZ, BLUES & FOLK

CLUB PASSIM

The area's premier folk music venue attracts both up-and-coming and well-established performers.
➕ C2 ✉ 47 Palmer Street, Cambridge ☎ 617/492 7679 🕐 Music Tue–Sun 🚇 Harvard

HOUSE OF BLUES

A well-equipped venue featuring live music and a very popular Sunday gospel group brunch.
➕ C3 ✉ 96 Winthrop Street, Cambridge ☎ 617/491 2583 🕐 Live shows from 10PM; brunch three sittings 🚇 Harvard

JOHNNY D'S

Good food and fine sounds, including blues and world music in Somerville's Davis Square, just north of Cambridge. Frequent performances by zydeco and Latin groups.
➕ Off map at 1C ✉ 17 Holland Street, Somerville ☎ 617/776 2004 🚇 Davis Square

REGATTABAR

First-class jazz acts in a pleasant bar in the Charles Hotel. Annual festival January through April.
➕ C3 ✉ 1 Bennett Street, Cambridge ☎ 617/864 1200, 617/876 7777 🕐 Closed Sun, Mon 🚇 Harvard Square

RYLES

Another Cambridge hotspot, in Inman Square, with food downstairs. Emphasis now on Latin jazz. Weekly learn-to-salsa Latin dance night.
➕ D3 ✉ 212 Hampshire Street, Cambridge ☎ 617/876 9330 🕐 Daily 7PM–1AM (Fri, Sat till 2AM), Sun brunch 10–3 🚇 Central then long walk or bus 83; Harvard then bus 69 along Cambridge Street

SCULLERS

Famous names perform great jazz in this bar at the Doubletree Suites Hotel, Tuesday to Saturday (and some Sundays). Book in advance.
➕ C4 ✉ 400 Soldiers Field Road at River Street Bridge ☎ 617/783 0811

MUSIC & DANCE CLUBS

AVALON

Combining live acts and dance, Avalon offers an international, alternative and house on Thursday and Friday, mainstream on Saturday, house on Sunday.
➕ E5 ✉ 15 Lansdowne Street ☎ 617/262 2424 🕐 Thu–Sun 10PM–2AM 🚇 Kenmore

AXIS

Next door to Avalon, and sharing a combined admission night with it on Sunday (gay night). Other nights feature house, soul, funk, alternative music.
➕ E5 ✉ 13 Lansdowne Street ☎ 617/262 2437 🕐 Thu–Mon 10PM–2AM 🚇 Kenmore

KARMA CLUB

Another Lansdowne Street favourite, offering DJ and live music. Joins forces with nearby Bill's Bar on Tuesday for dance.
➕ E5 ✉ 9 Lansdowne Street ☎ 617/421 9595 🕐 Tue–Sun 10PM–2AM 🚇 Kenmore

M-80

Trendy spot for chic ravers with a deafeningly powerful sound system.

✚ C5 ✉ 969 Commonwealth Avenue ☎ 617/562 8800 ◷ Wed; Fri; Sat Ⓜ Pleasant Street (green line B)

RHYTHM & SPICE CARIBBEAN BAR & GRILL

A restaurant/club near MIT that attracts a multi-racial mix of students and professionals. After sampling Jamaican jerk chicken, curried goat or rotis, you can stick around for reggae, soca and other island rhythms. Calypso brunch on Sundays.

✚ E4 ✉ 315 Massachusetts Avenue (near Main Street) ☎ 617/497 0977 ◷ Music Fri–Sat 10:30PM–1AM; Sun brunch noon–3 Ⓜ Central, then walk

THE ROXY

In the Theater District, one of the city's largest nightclub hosts world music events and dance parties.

✚ G5 ✉ 279 Tremont Street ☎ 617/338 7699 ◷ Thu 10PM–2AM; Fri, Sat 9PM–2AM Ⓜ Boylston

BARS, COMEDY & GAMES

BOSTON BILLIARD CLUB

Popular Fenway Park hangout for pool addicts.

✚ D6 ✉ 126 Brookline Avenue ☎ 617/536–POOL ◷ Noon–2AM Ⓜ Kenmore

COMEDY CONNECTION

A first-class comedy club with shows every night, two on Friday and Saturday. Book ahead.

✚ dIII; H4 ✉ Faneuil Hall Marketplace ☎ 617/248 9700 ◷ Shows Mon–Wed 8PM; Thu 8:30PM; Fri, Sat 8, 10:15PM; Sun 7PM Ⓜ State, Government Center

DICK DOHERTY'S COMEDY VAULT

A leading comedy club, set in a former bank vault.

✚ G5 ✉ 124 Boylston Street ☎ 617/482 0110 ◷ Shows Thu–Sun Ⓜ Boylston

IMPROV ASYLUM

Improvisational comedy at a North End basement cabaret-style theatre.

✚ dII; H4 ✉ 216 Hanover Street ☎ 617/263 6887 ◷ Shows Thu–Sat Ⓜ Haymarket

JILLIAN'S

An essential stop for virtual reality and pool fans; virtual sports, 200 high-tech games, 50 pool tables, plus five bars and bistro-style food.

✚ E6 ✉ 145 Ipswich Street ☎ 617/437 0300 ◷ Pool Hall Mon–Sat 11AM–2AM; Sun noon–2AM. Games Mon–Fri 5PM–2AM; Sat 11AM–2AM; Sun noon–2AM Ⓜ Kenmore

NICK'S COMEDY STOP

A well-loved Theater District comedy club with local stars and would-be stars on stage.

✚ G5 ✉ 100 Warrenton Street ☎ 617/482 0930 ◷ Shows Thu–Sat 8:30, but changes all the time – call for current shows schedule Ⓜ Boylston

Nightlife and harbour cruises

Odyssey

Operates evening cruises on a 600-passenger yacht, plus a Sunday jazz brunch and weekday lunches (both 10:45–1:30).

✉ Atlantic Avenue; sails from Rowes Wharf ☎ 617/654 9710 or 800/946 7245 ◷ Call for specific sailing schedule; advance booking required

The Spirit of Boston

Has live bands and shows on its dinner dance cruises.

✉ Northern Avenue; sails from World Trade Center ☎ 617/748 1450 ◷ Lunch cruises Tue–Sun; dinner cruises most evenings, except Mon

LUXURY HOTELS

Prices

For a standard double room in a luxury hotel expect to pay from $150–$435 in low season to $355–$625 in high season. However, with prices varying according to days of the week and the time of year, some hotel rates may lie in the mid-range category, opposite. For hotels in all price categories, always be sure to ask if there are any special deals: some hotels offer winter rates and/or theatre weekends. If you have children, ask about family packages. Note also that many luxury and mid-range hotels have restaurants which are listed on pages 62–63.

Health and fitness

Unless otherwise noted, all hotels listed on this page and on page 85 either have fitness centres and pools within the hotel, or offer use of nearby health spas (sometimes there is a fee to pay for these).

Business facilities

The luxury and mid-range hotels listed here generally offer standard business facilities.

BOSTON HARBOUR

Modern, elegant and on the waterfront, where the airport shuttle ferry docks. It's worth paying a little more for harbour views. Good restaurant, with views to match.

➕ eIV; J4 ✉ 70 Rowes Wharf ☎ 617/439 7000 or 800/752 7077, fax 617/330 9450 Ⓣ Aquarium

CHARLES

A modern luxury hotel in Harvard Square. Home of Rialto, Henrietta's Table and Regatta bar jazz club.

➕ C3 ✉ One Bennett Street, Cambridge ☎ 617/864 1200 or 800/882 1818, fax 617/864 5715 Ⓣ Harvard

COPLEY SQUARE

Turn-of-the-century hotel with European flavour. For Café Budapest. No fitness centre or pool.

➕ F5 ✉ 47 Huntington Avenue ☎ 617/536 9000 or 800/225 7062, fax 617/267 3547 Ⓣ Copley

FAIRMOUNT COPLEY PLAZA

A 'grand dame' of Boston, famed for its sumptuous decor (if you don't stay here, at least take a tour).

➕ F5 ✉ 138 St James Avenue ☎ 617/267 5300 or 800/527 4727, 800/795 3906, fax 617/247 6681 Ⓣ Copley

FOUR SEASONS

All you could ask for in elegance and service. Aujourd'hui and Bristol restaurants.

➕ G5 ✉ 200 Boylston Street ☎ 617/338 4400 or 800/332 3442, fax 617/351 2051 Ⓣ Arlington

LE MERIDIEN

Historic 1920s building in the heart of the Financial District. Julien restaurant.

➕ dIV; H4 ✉ 250 Franklin Street (Post Office Square) ☎ 617/451 1900 or 800/543 4300, fax 617/423 2844 Ⓣ State, Downtown Crossing

LENOX

Built in 1900, with many period details preserved, this independent is one of the best.

➕ F5 ✉ 710 Boylston Street ☎ 617/536 5300 or 800/225 7676, fax 617/266 7905 Ⓣ Copley

REGAL BOSTONIAN

More intimate than some, offers comfort without glitz. Seasons Restaurant.

➕ dIII; H4 ✉ Faneuil Hall Marketplace ☎ 617/523 3600 or 800/343 0922, fax 617/523 2454 Ⓣ State, Government Center

RITZ-CARLTON

The ultimate in graciousness. Stop in the lounge for tea, the bar for martinis, the dining room for dinner, or the café for after-theatre. Overlooks Newbury Street and the Public Garden.

➕ aV; G5 ✉ 15 Arlington Street ☎ 617/536 5700 or 800/241 3333; fax 617/5536 9340 Ⓣ Arlington

WESTIN

Thirty six storeys; handsome rooms; direct access to Copley Place mall. Jazz nights in the Turner Fisheries Bar.

➕ F5 ✉ 10 Huntington Avenue ☎ 617/262 9600 or 800/228 3000; fax 617/424 7483 Ⓣ Copley

MID-RANGE HOTELS

BACK BAY HILTON

Standard Hilton comfort. Convenient to the Pru/Hynes Centers.

✚ F6 ✉ 40 Dalton Street ☎ 617/236 1100 or 800/874 0663, fax 617/867 6139 ♿ Prudential, Hynes/ICA

BOSTON PARK PLAZA & TOWERS

Elegant hotel built in 1927. Near the Public Garden and Theater District. Family friendly.

✚ G5 ✉ 64 Arlington Street ☎ 617/426 2000 or 800/225 2008, fax 617/423 1708 ♿ Arlington

COLONNADE

Small independent hotel near the Pru Center and Symphony Hall. Home of Brasserie Jo restaurant.

✚ F6 ✉ 120 Huntington Avenue ☎ 617/424 7000 or 800/962 3030, fax 617/424 1717 ♿ Prudential

ELIOT

Elegance, comfort and good value (though not the best location on Commonwealth Avenue). An all-suites hotel, each with a living room and kitchenette. Home of Clio restaurant.

✚ E5 ✉ 370 Commonwealth Avenue ☎ 617/267 1607 or 800/44 ELIOT, fax 617/536 9114 ♿ Hynes/ICA

MARRIOTT COPLEY PLACE

A 38-floor hotel in Copley Place mall with a covered walkway to Pru/Hynes. Good value winter deals.

✚ F6 ✉ 110 Huntington Avenue ☎ 617/236 5800 or 800/228 9290 fax 617/578 4685 ♿ Prudential, Copley

MARRIOTT LONG WHARF

Built like an ocean liner, this hotel has a fine harbourside position. Close to Faneuil. May be more expensive than Marriott Copley Place.

✚ elll; J4 ✉ 296 State Street (Long Wharf) ☎ 617/227 0800 or 800/228 9290, fax 617/227 2867 ♿ Aquarium

OMNI PARKER HOUSE

A rather staid 19th-century establishment, a block from Boston Common. Chefs from this hotel invented two of the mainstays of traditional American cooking – the Parker House roll and Boston cream pie.

✚ clV; H4 ✉ 60 School Street ☎ 617/227 8600 or 800/843 6644, fax 617/742 5729 ♿ Park

SHERATON & SHERATON TOWERS

A large one, in the Pru Mall/Hynes Convention Center. The Towers is the more luxurious; butlers available on request.

✚ F6 ✉ Prudential Center, 39 Dalton Street ☎ 617/236 2000 or 800/325 3535, fax 617/236 6061 ♿ Prudential, Hynes/ICA

SWISSÔTEL

The plain, modern façade belies classic European elegance inside. Exemplary service and a downtown location make it a good choice for business or sightseeing.

✚ cV; H5 ✉ 1 Avenue de Lafayette ☎ 617/451 2600 or 800/621 9200, fax 617/451 2198 ♿ Downtown Crossing

Prices

For a standard double room in a mid-range hotel, expect to pay from $130–$235 in low season to $260–$335 in high season (► 84 panel).

In Cambridge

Mid-range options include:

Hyatt Regency

On the Charles river, with a revolving rooftop lounge.

✉ 575 Memorial Drive ☎ 617/492 1234 or 800/233 1234, fax 617/491 6906

A Cambridge House

An old bed-and-breakfast inn in north Cambridge.

✉ 2218 Massachusetts Avenue ☎ 617/491 6300 or 800/232 9989, fax 617/868 2848

Out of town

When every hotel room in Boston seems to be taken up with conventioneers – as is often the case – consider staying in towns such as Quincy, Concord or Salem, all charming places only 30 to 40 minutes from Boston and served by regular train services. For help with booking, contact:

DestINNations

✉ 572 Route 28, West Yarmouth MA 02673 ☎ 617/508 790 0577 or 800/333 4667, fax 617/508 790 0565

BUDGET ACCOMMODATION

Prices

You should get a double room in the majority of the establishments listed here for under $100; expect to pay around $130–$200 in high season. Double occupancy in bed-and-breakfast accommodation range from $80 to $160.

Bed & Breakfast and self-catering

There is a shortage of budget-priced hotels with character in Boston. As a pleasant alternative consider a bed and breakfast (many are in very comfortable private homes) or self-catering. Try:

Bed & Breakfast Agency of Boston

A helpful and friendly agency that will find you accommodation in historic houses and restored waterfront lofts. Nightly, weekly, monthly and winter rates (✉ 47 Commercial Wharf ☎ 617/720 3540 or 800/248 9262, fax 617/523 5761).

BEST WESTERN

Near medical complexes and Fenway Park.
➕ D7 ✉ 342 Longwood Avenue ☎ 617/731 4700 or 800/528 1234, fax 617/731 6273 🚇 Green line D to Longwood

BOSTON INTERNATIONAL YOUTH HOSTEL

Dormitories, cooking facilities available.
➕ E6 ✉ 12 Hemenway Street ☎ 617/536 9455, fax 617/424 6558 🚇 Hynes/ICA

CHANDLER INN

Cheap basic hotel in the attractive South End district. Near Copley/Pru.
➕ G6 ✉ 26 Chandler Street ☎ 617/482 3450 or 800/842 3450, fax 617/542 3428 🚇 Back Bay

HOLIDAY INN

A functional base at the foot of Beacon Hill's north slope. Outdoor pool.
➕ bIII; G4 ✉ 5 Blossom Street ☎ 617/742 7630 or 800/ HOLIDAY, fax 617/742 4192 🚇 Charles, Bowdoin

HOWARD JOHNSON LODGE FENWAY

Convenient to Red Sox games and art galleries.
➕ E6 ✉ 1271 Boylston Street ☎ 617/267 8300 or 800/654 2000, fax 617/267 2763 🚇 Kenmore

JOHN JEFFRIES HOUSE

Four-storey brick inn on Beacon Hill; 46 mostly tiny rooms. The two-room suites are better value.
➕ aIII; G4 ✉ 14 David Mugar Way (formerly Embankment Road) at Charles Circle

☎ 617/367 1866, fax 617/742 0313 🚇 Charles

MARY PRENTISS INN

An antique-filled bed and breakfast with modern amenities between Harvard and Porter squares. Breakfast is on the deck in summer.
➕ C1 ✉ 6 Prentiss Street, Cambridge ☎ 617/661 2929, fax 617/661 5989 🚇 Porter

NEWBURY GUEST HOUSE

Victorian-style rooms (32) in three connected redbrick terraces. Excellent value, popular; book well ahead.
➕ F5 ✉ 261 Newbury Street ☎ 617/437 7666 or 800/437 7668, fax 617/262 4243 🚇 Copley, Hynes/ICA

SUSSE CHALET

Cheaper option 3 miles south of town. Outdoor pool, bowling alley nearby.
➕ Off map at H10 ✉ 900 Morrissey Boulevard ☎ 617/ 287 9200 or 800/886 0056, fax 617/282 2365 🚇 JFK, then half-hourly hotel shuttle bus 7AM–9PM

TREMONT HOUSE

Theater District 1920s hotel. Chandeliers in public areas, modern furnishings in bedrooms.
➕ G5 ✉ 275 Tremont Street ☎ 617/426 1400 or 800/331 9998, fax 617/423 0374 🚇 Boylston

YMCA CENTRAL

Shared bathrooms – but maid service. In summer open to anyone over 18; in school year to men only.
➕ E6 ✉ 316 Huntington Avenue ☎ 617/536 7800 🚇 Green line E to Northeastern

BOSTON
travel facts

Arriving & Departing   88–89

Essential Facts   89–91

Public Transport   91–92

Driving & Car Hire   92–93

Media &
    Communications   93

Emergencies   93

ARRIVING & DEPARTING

Before you go

- All visitors to the US must show a full and valid passport.
- UK citizens and other visitors from countries that belong to the Visa Waiver Program can enter the US without a visa, but you must have a return or onward ticket, and you must not stay longer than 90 days.
- Before landing in the US, you will be given a green form – the Non-Immigrant Visa Waiver form – to fill in. This confirms that your visit is for pleasure and not for illicit or sinister purposes.

When to go

- Boston is pretty in spring, especially when the magnolias in the Back Bay are in full bloom. Tourist-wise, it's relatively quiet, but the city is a popular conference venue and hotel space can be snapped up quickly.
- Peak visiting is summer (around graduation time) and autumn (particularly October when Boston serves as a base for trips to see New England's glorious fall foliage) when there are plenty of events and festivals.
- The six weeks between Thanksgiving and New Year is another lovely time to visit. The Public Garden looks like something out of a fairy tale with millions of tiny lights in the trees, and there are plenty of seasonal festivities.
- Avoid travelling on the Wednesday before and the Sunday after Thanksgiving Day (4th Thursday in November), when all America is on the move.

Climate

- Spring (April to May), although unpredictable, can be wonderful, with cool nights and fresh days ranging from 15° to 20°C.
- Boston enjoys warm summers, peaking in July, when the temperatures creep towards 30°C.
- Autumn is generally mild, with September temperatures hovering in the early 20s°C.
- Winters are cold; snow often falls December to February/March and temperatures plummet to -3°C.

Arriving by air

- Logan Airport, 3 miles from downtown Boston, has five terminals connected by walkways, free shuttle buses, restaurants, hotels and other facilities.
- Buses marked 'Massport Shuttle' carry passengers free to the Airport T (underground) station on the Blue line; from here it's a few minutes' journey to downtown Boston (85¢) 🚇 Shuttle bus every 8–12 minutes, 5:30AM–1AM.
- The Airport Water Shuttle runs between Logan and Rowes Wharf in the Financial District – it's an exciting way to arrive ☎ 617/330 8680 🚇 Journey time 10 minutes. Runs every 15 minutes Mon–Fri 6AM–8PM; every 30 minutes Fri 8AM–11PM, Sat 10AM–11PM, Sun 10AM–8PM. No service 4 Jul, Thanksgiving Day, 25 Dec and 1 Jan 🚇 $10.
- The on-call City Water Taxi runs from the airport to ten waterfront locations ☎ 617/422 0392 🚇 Apr to mid-Oct 7AM–7PM 🚇 $10.
- Harbor Express operates between Logan, Long Wharf and Quincy 🚇 Mon–Fri 5AM–10:35PM; Sat, Sun 6AM–9:45PM. Times vary. No service Thanksgiving Day, 25 Dec 🚇 Logan–Long Wharf $10.
- Metered taxis are available at all terminals 🚇 Average to downtown $10–18. Included in this is the toll the driver pays for using the tunnel under the harbour; you may be handed the receipt.
- Airport van services can be a

cheaper option than a taxi if you are travelling alone. The shared minibus takes you to your destination but picks up and drops off passengers en route. Fare is per-person (average $8 to downtown or Back Bay, $15–16 to Cambridge). US Shuttle ☎ 617/894 3100 (call from the airport or reserve 24 to 48 hours ahead.)

- An Airport Handicap Van offers a free service between all airport locations. Use the free 'Van Phone' in the baggage claim area.

Arriving by bus

- Greyhound and Peter Pan buses travel frequently between New York and Boston, arriving at South station.
- Greyhound buses ☎ 800/231 2222
- Peter Pan buses ☎ 617/482 6620.

Arriving by car

- From the west, Route I-90, the Massachusetts Turnpike, runs into Boston with exits leading to Cambridge, Storrow Drive (for Fenway, Kenmore Square, and Boston Common), the Back Bay, Downtown, and I-93 (the Expressway).
- From the south, I-93 has exits for Chinatown, South station, Downtown, and for the Callahan Tunnel to the airport.
- Routes US1 and I-93 lead in from the north with exits marked Storrow Drive (for Cambridge and Boston Common), High Street (for Downtown), and Kneeland Street (for Chinatown and the Theater District).

Arriving by train

- Amtrak services ☎ 617/482 3660 run almost hourly between Boston and New York, Philadelphia, and Washington, DC, arriving at South station.

- The high-speed service between New York to Boston takes two and three-quarter hours.

Customs regulations

- Visitors aged 21 or more may import duty-free: 200 cigarettes or 50 cigars or 2kg of tobacco; 1 litre (1 US quart) of alcohol; and gifts up to $100 in value.
- Restricted import items include meat, seeds, plants and fruit.

ESSENTIAL FACTS

Alcohol

- It is illegal to drink alcohol in public places such as the T or the street.
- It is illegal to sell alcohol to under 21s. Alcohol is not sold in shops on Sundays or after 11PM Monday to Saturday.

Electricity

- The US supply is 110 volts AC, so European shavers and hair-driers work but may be a bit feeble.
- US plugs have two pins – European three-pin appliances will need adaptors.

Etiquette

- In restaurants a 5 per cent meal tax is added to the bill. A tip of 15 to 20 per cent is usually expected.
- Tip 15 per cent for taxis and $1 to $1.50 a bag for airport and hotel porters.
- Some restaurants require jackets and ties for men, but on the whole evening meals are informal affairs.

Insurance

- It is vital that travel insurance covers medical expenses (which can be horrendously high in the US), in addition to accident, trip cancellation, baggage loss and theft.
- Check that your policy covers any

continuing treatment for a chronic condition and whether you need to provide a doctor's certificate.

Money matters

- The unit of currency is the dollar (= 100 cents). Notes (bills) come in denominations of $1, $5, $10, $20, $50 and $100; coins are 25¢ (a quarter), 10¢ (a dime), 5¢ (a nickel).
- Nearly all banks have cashpoints (Automatic Teller Machines; ATMs). Cards registered in other countries that are linked to the Cirrus or Plus networks are accepted. Before leaving, check which network your cards are linked to and ensure your PIN is valid in the US, where six-figure numbers are the norm.
- Credit cards are a widely accepted and are secure alternative to cash.
- US dollar traveller's cheques function like cash virtually everywhere, so you get change if what you are buying costs less than the cheque is worth. This is a handy way of getting cash. $20 and $50 denominations are the most useful.
- Money and traveller's cheques can be exchanged at most banks (check commisions as they can be high) and many travel centres in central Boston.
- Some businesses may ask for photo identification (such as a passport) before cashing traveller's cheques.

Opening hours

- Banks: Mon–Fri 9–3; Thu 9–5 or later; Sat 9–2.
- Shops: Mon–Sat 10–6 or later. Closed Sunday mornings.
- Museums and sights: unless otherwise stated, all sights mentioned in this book close on Thanksgiving and Christmas.
- Businesses: Mon–Fri 8 or 9–5.

Public holidays

- 1 Jan (New Year's Day); 3rd Mon in Jan (Martin Luther King Day); 3rd Mon in Feb (President's Day); last Mon in May (Memorial Day); 4 July (Independence Day); 1st Mon in Sep (Labor Day); 2nd Mon in Oct (Columbus Day); 11 Nov (Veterans Day); 4th Thu in Nov (Thanksgiving Day); 25 Dec (Christmas Day).
- Boston also celebrates: 17 Mar (Evacuation Day); 3rd Mon in Apr (Patriots Day); 17 Jun (Bunker Hill Day).

Sensible precautions

- Boston is a remarkably safe city, however, it is advisable to avoid Boston Common and the southern half of Washington Street after dark.
- Be aware of the people and activities around you, especially at night or in quiet areas.
- Keep your wallet or purse tucked out-of-sight and don't carry valuables or cash openly.

Smoking

- Smoking is banned in many public places, including the T. Some hotels have no-smoking floors. By law smoking is banned in restaurants unless there is a separate, enclosed seating area.
- Cambridge is by law smoke-free.

Student travellers

- Carriers of an ISIC (International Student Identity Card) may get discounts at some museums and theatres.
- Members of the Youth Hostel Association of England and Wales ✉ Trevelyan House, 8 St Stephen's Hill, St Albans, Herts AL1 2DY ☎ 01727 855215 can use youth hostels.
- Information on student hostels within the US can be obtained

from Hostelling International-American Youth Hostels ✉ PO Box 37613, WAshington, DC 20013-7613 ☎ 202/783 6161 or 800/444 6111.

Tickets

- The nine-day Boston CityPass (adult $26.50; seniors and youth discounts) gives half-price admission to six key sights: the Museum of Fine Arts, the Museum of Science, the New England Aquarium, the Isabella Stewart Gardner Museum, the John F Kennedy Library and Museum, and the John Hancoock Observatory. Available from the above or at the visitor information centres on Boston Common or in the Prudential Center.
- For tickets for performing arts and sports events, museums and trolley tours (► 80).
- For the public transport MBTA Visitor Passport see under Public Transport.

Time differences

- Boston is in the Eastern Time Zone, 5 hours behind Greenwich Mean Time.
- Clocks are put one hour forward (Daylight Saving Time) between the first Saturday in April and the last Saturday in October.

Toilets

- These are few and far between downtown. There are some in the Visitor Center in State Street, in Faneuil Hall Marketplace, in Old South Meeting House, and on Boston Common. Best bets: department stores, hotels and, at a pinch, bars/restaurants; you should buy a drink before you use the lavatory in a bar.

Tourist Offices

- Greater Boston Convention & Visitors Bureau Inc ✉ 2 Copley Place, Suite 105, Boston, MA 02116-6501 ☎ 617/536 4100, fax 617/424 7664; website: www.boston.usa.com
- Massachusetts Office of Travel & Tourism ✉ State Transportation, 10 Park Plaza, Suite 4510, Boston, MA 02116 ☎ 617/727 3201, fax 617/973 8525; website: www.massvacation.com
- Boston National Historical Park Visitor Center ✉ 15 State Street, opposite Old State House ☎ 617/242 5642
- Boston Common Information Center ✉ Tremont Street ☎ 617/536 4100
- Cambridge Visitor Information ✉ Harvard Square, Cambridge ☎ 617/497 1630
- In the UK: Massachusetts Office of Travel & Tourism ✉ Molasses House, Clove Hitch Quay, Plantation Wharf, York Place, London SW11 3TN ☎ 020 7978 5233.

Visitors with disabilities

- Boston is well equipped for visitors with disabilities. Public buildings, car parks and underground stations provide wheelchair access. Some hotels have specially designed rooms.
- For advice and information contact the Information Center for Individuals with Disabilities ✉ PO Box 750119, Arlington Heights, MA 02475 ☎ 617/450 9888 or (in Massachusetts) 800/642 0249
- In the UK contact RADAR ✉ 62 Gower Street, London W1 ☎ 020 7250 3222
- In Ireland contact the Disabled Drivers Association of Ireland or the Irish Association of Physically Handicapped People, Ballindine, Co Mayo.

PUBLIC TRANSPORT

Boats

- The Airport Water Shuttle and the City Water Taxi sail regularly across Boston Harbor (► 88).

- Commuter boats are operated by Mass Bay Lines ✉ 60 Rowes Wharf ☎ 617/542 8000

- MBTA Hingham Commuter Boat operates between Hingham Shipyard and Rowes Wharf, with connections to Logan Airport via the Airport Water Shuttle ☎ 800/262 3355

- For ferry services to Charlestown (► 43).

Buses

- Very few bus routes run into downtown Boston; most visitors find the T quicker and easier.

- Buses travel further out into the suburbs than the T and are used mainly by commuters.

- Passengers must have the exact change (60¢) or an MTBA token.

Taxis

- Taxis can be hailed on the street or found at hotels and taxi stands.

- 24-hour taxi services include: Checker Cab Co ☎ 617/497 9000 Metrocab Cab ☎ 617/242 8000 Town Taxis ☎ 617/536 5000.

Trains

- MBTA commuter trains leave from North station for destinations west and north, including Concord, Lowell, and the North shore towns of Salem, Manchester, Gloucester, Rockport and Ipswich. South station serves the South shore, Plymouth and Providence.

The underground (subway – T)

- Known simply as the T, the MBTA (Massachusetts Bay Transportation Authority) runs under- and over-ground trains along four 'rapid transit' lines: Red, Green, Orange and Blue, all of which meet in

downtown Boston. The T is clean, efficient, safe, and easy to use. 'Inbound' and 'Outbound' refer to the direction in relation to Park Street station.

- Trains run between 5AM (later on Sun) and 12:45AM.

- Tokens (85¢) can be bought at station kiosks. Buy several at once to save time. One token covers any trip out to the suburbs, but the journey back can cost more.

- MBTA Visitor Passports give unlimited travel for one, three, or seven days (£$5, $9, $18) available at the visitor information centres on Boston Common and at the Shops at the Prudential Center (Center Court) 🕓 Daily 9–5.

- Free maps of MTBA routes are available at the Park Street station information kiosk. Some maps do not show all stops on the Green line branches.

DRIVING & CAR HIRE

Car hire

- Drivers must generally be at least 21; many companies put the minimum age at 25 or charge extra for those aged between 21 and 25.

- There is a 5 per cent tax on car hire.

- Car hire companies in Boston: Avis ☎ 800/331 1212 Budget ☎ 800/527 0700 Dollar ☎ 800/800 4000 Hertz ☎ 800/654 3131.

Driving

- Driving and parking in Boston is a nightmare. Use public transport and avoid parking problems. A car is only likely to be useful for trips out of Boston (but see Trains).

- A full valid UK or EU driving licence is required (an international driving permit is not accepted alone). Carry it with you.

- The speed limits on the major highways is between 55 and 65mph; elsewhere it is between 30 and 45mph.
- All front seat passengers must wear a seat belt. Children under 12 must sit in the back and use an approved car seat or safety belt.
- You may turn right at a red traffic light if the road ahead is clear.
- Park only in legal spots or you will be towed. Park in the direction of the traffic.
- Drink/driving laws are very strict. Never drive after drinking; don't keep opened alcohol in the car.

MEDIA & COMMUNICATIONS

Magazines & newspapers
- Free tourist-aimed magazines are found in hotel lobbies; their discount coupons can save money on sightseeing and food.
- The newsstand at Harvard Square T station, Cambridge, sells a range of international newspapers and magazines.
- Cultural and entertainment lists can be found in the dailies: the *Boston Globe* (Thursday) and the less liberal *Boston Herald* (Friday).
- Weekly *Boston Phoenix* also carries a guide to what's on (Thursday).
- Monthly *Boston Magazine* reviews the Boston scene and gives coveted awards to restaurants.

Post Offices
- The most useful post offices for visitors are in the Prudential Center and Faneuil Hall.
- Letter boxes are grey/blue and have swing-top lids.

Telephones
- The Boston area code is 617

(included throughout this book). To dial outside the area (including free phone 800 numbers), dial 1 then the area code and number.

- Payphones take 5¢, 10¢ and 25¢ coins and phone cards, which can be recharged using a credit card.
- Local calls cost 25 or 30¢.
- International operator ☎ 1 800/874 4000; UK country code: 01144; Ireland country code: 011353.

Television & radio
- TV: ABC Channel 5; CBS Channel 4; NBC Channel 7; PBS Channels 2 and 44; 68 is a local sports channel.
- Local radio FM stations: WGBH 89.7 and WBUR 90.9.

EMERGENCIES

Consulates
- Great Britain ✉ 600 Atlantic Avenue ☎ 617/248 9555.
- Ireland ✉ 535 Boylston Street ☎ 617/267 9330.

Emergency phone numbers
- Ambulance, fire, police ☎ 911
- Dental emergency ☎ 617/636 6828
- Massachusetts General Hospital ☎ 617/726 2000
- Late-night pharmacies: CVS ✉ Porter Square (36 White Street near Massachusetts Avenue), Cambridge ☎ 617/876 5519 🕐 Till midnight. ✉ 155 Charles Street, Boston ☎ 617/523 1028 🕐 24 hours.

Lost property
- To report lost credit cards: American Express ☎ 800/528 2121 Diners Club/Carte Blanche ☎ 800/234 6377, MasterCard ☎ 800/826 2181, Visa ☎ 800/227 6811
- To report lost traveller's cheques: American Express ☎ 800/221 7282 Thomas Cook ☎ 800/223 7373.

INDEX

A

academia 9
accommodation 84–86
Adams, Sam 55
African Meeting House 53, 60
airport 88
alcohol 89
Ames Building 54
antique shops 76
architecture 6, 54
Arnold Arboretum 57
art galleries, commercial 70
Arthur M Sackler Museum 26

B

Back Bay 14, 18, 33
Back Bay Fens 57
banks 90
bars 83
baseball 58
basketball 58
Beacon Hill 14, 16, 35
bed and breakfast 86
bike hire 74
biking 58
Black Heritage Trail 19, 53
boat shuttles 91
boat trips 19, 46, 51, 57
book and music shops 75
Boott Cotton Mills Museum 21
Boston Athenaeum 39
Boston Common 9, 36, 60
Boston firsts 9
Boston Harbor Islands 47
Boston Marathon 58
Boston nicknames 9
Boston Pops 60, 78
Boston Public Library 31, 60
Boston Tea Party 12
Boston Tea Party Ship and Museum 52
Botanical Museum 26
Brahmins 6, 8, 9, 35
Brattle House 24
Brattle Street 24
breweries and brewpubs 66
Brookline 52
Bulfinch, Charles 12, 35, 37, 38, 42, 53
Bunker Hill Monument 43, 55
burial grounds 56
Busch-Reisinger Museum 26
buses 92

buses, long-distance 89

C

Cambridge 9, 15, 25–26, 50, 56, 85
canoeing, kayaking and sailing 58
car hire 92
Carpenter Center for the Visual Arts 25
cashpoints 90
Charles River Esplanade 18, 57, 60
Charlestown Navy Yard 43
children
    dining with 68
    entertainment 59
Children's Museum 59, 60
Chinatown 50
choral and early music groups 78
cinema 81
classical music 60, 78–79
climate 88
clothes shops 72–73
clubs 82–83
coffee and tea 68–69
comedy clubs 83
Commonwealth Avenue 33
Commonwealth Museum 60
communications 93
concert halls 78
Concord 20
USS *Constitution* 43, 60
Consulates 93
Copp's Hill Burying Ground 56
crafts and gifts 76–77
credit cards 90, 93
Curley, James 55
Custom House Tower 54

D

daily life 8
dance 79
department stores, malls 71
Dexter Pratt House 24
disabilities, visitors with 91
Downtown Crossing 50, 70
Duck Tours 19
driving to Boston 89
Durgin Park Dining Rooms 42, 62

E

eating out 62–69, 89
Emerald Necklace 57

emergencies 93
emergency phone numbers 93
entertainment 78–83
etiquette 89
evening strolls 18
excursions 20–21

F

factory outlets 71
Faneuil Hall and Marketplace 18, 42, 60, 70
Federal Reserve Bank & Boston cultural events 60
Fenway 15, 50, 58
festivals and events 22, 60
Filene's Basement 72
Financial District 51
First Church of Christ, Scientist 29, 60
FleetCenter 51, 58
Fogg Art Museum 26
food shops 77
Franklin Park Zoo 59
Frederick Law Olmsted National Historic Site 52
free and cheap attractions 60
Freedom Trail 6, 14, 17, 19

G

Georges Island 47
Gibson House Museum 52
Government Center 51

H

harbour cruises 19, 83
Harrison Gray Otis House 37
Hart Nautical Collection 53
Harvard Square 18, 25, 60, 70
Harvard University 25
Museums 26, 60
Head of the Charles Regatta 58
historic houses 52–53
holidays, national 90
hotels 84–86
history 10–12
household goods 76–77
'the Hub' 7, 9

I

ice hockey 58

in-line skating 58, 74
Institute of Contemporary Art (ICA) 52, 60
insurance 89
Isabella Stewart Gardner Museum 27, 79
itineraries 14–15

J

Jamaica Pond 57
JFK National Historic Site 52
jogging 58
John F Kennedy Library and Museum 48
John Hancock Tower and Observatory 30

K

Kennedy, J F 12, 48, 52
King's Chapel and Burying Ground 56

L

Leather District 51
Little Italy 44
Longfellow House 24
lost property 93
Louisburg Square 35
Lowell 20–21

M

Make Way for Ducklings 36, 59
Mapparium 29, 60
maps 75
markets 42, 76
Massachusetts State House 38, 60
Mayflower II 21
media 93
medical treatment 93
MIT 53, 54, 55
MIT museums 53
money 90
Mount Auburn Cemetery 56
Mugar Omni Theater 34
Museum of Afro-American History 53
Museum of Fine Arts (MFA) 28, 60, 79, 81
Museum of Science 34
Museum of Transportation 52
Museums of Cultural and Natural History 26
museums and galleries 52–53

music hall entertainment 81

N

New England Aquarium 46
New England Conservatory 60, 78
New England cuisine 66
New England Holocaust Memorial 55
Newbury Street 33, 70
newspapers and magazines 93
Nichols House Museum 53
North End 44
North End Market Towns 19

O

Old Granary Burying Ground 56
Old North Church 44
Old South Meeting House 40
Old State House 41
Old West End 51
Olmsted, Frederick Law 52, 57
opening hours 70, 90
opera 79
outdoor activities 58
Outlet shopping 71

P

Park Street Church 56
parks and open spaces 57, 60
Paul Revere House 45
Peabody Essex Museum 21
Peabody Museum 26
Planetarium 34
Playgrounds 59
Plimoth Plantation 21
Plymouth 21
Post Office Square 54
precautions, sensible 90
Prudential Tower 30
Public Garden 36, 59, 60
public transport 91–92
puppet theatre 80

Q

Quilt Museum 21

R

Radcliffe College 25
restaurants 62–67, 89
Revere, Paul 12, 38, 44, 45, 55, 56
Robert Gould Shaw Monument 55
rollerblading 58, 74

S

Sacred Cod 38
safety 90
St Stephen's Church 56
Salem 21
sales tax 70
seafood 64
Sears Building 54
self-catering 86
shoes and outdoor gear 74
shopping 70–77
shopping districts 70–71
sightseeing, organised 19
skating 58, 74
smoking etiquette 90
South End 51
SPNEA 37
sport 58
Sports Museum of New England 21
statistics 9
statues, monuments and sculptures 55
Stoughton House 24
street entertainment 60
student travellers 90
subway (T) 92
subway art 55
Swan Boats 36

T

taxes 70, 89, 92
taxis 92
telephones 93
television and radio 93
Theater District 50
the T (underground) 92
tickets 58, 80, 91
time differences 91
tipping 89
topography 9
tours 19
tourist offices 91
train services 89, 92
travelling to Boston 88–89
Trinity Church 32, 60, 79
trolley tours 19

V

vegetarian dining 67

W

walks 16–18, 51
Waterfront 18, 51, 82
whalewatching 19
Whistler House 21

CityPack
Boston

Written by   Sue Gordon
Edited, designed and produced by AA Publishing
Maps   © The Automobile Association 1997, 1999
Fold-out map © RV Reise- und Verkehrsverlag Munich · Stuttgart
© Cartography: GeoData

© The Automobile Association 1997, 1999
Reprinted Nov 1998 and Mar 1999. Revised second edition 1999.

ISBN 0 7495 2216 X

Published by AA Publishing (a trading name of Automobile Association Developments Limited, whose registered office is Norfolk House, Priestley Road, Basingstoke, Hampshire RG24 9NY. Registered number 1878835).

Colour separation by Daylight Colour Art Pte Ltd, Singapore
Printed and bound by Dai Nippon Printing Co (Hong Kong) Ltd.

Acknowledgements

The author would like to thank the following for their assistance in preparing this book: Carolyn Heller, British Airways, Greater Boston Convention & Visitors Bureau, Discover New England and Ferne Mintz of Bed & Breakfast Agency of Boston.
The Automobile Association wishes to thank the following photographers, libraries and associations in the preparation of this book:
Boston Athenaeum 39 (Photograph by Peter Vanderwarker. Collection of the Boston Athenaeum); The Bridgeman Art Library 28b *Long Branch* (detail) by Winslow Homer (1836–1910) Museum of Fine Arts, Boston, Massachusetts; Mary Evans Picture Library 12; S. Gordon 45a, 51; Harvard University Art Museums 26a (Courtesy of the Fogg Art Museum), 26b Gift of Paul J. Sachs in honour of Edward W. Forbe's thirtieth year as Director of the Fogg Museum; R. Holmes 25a, 44a; Index Stock Imagery/Kindra Clineff 47; John F. Kennedy Library & Museum 48b (Robert Schoen); MIT Museums 53 (The Harold E. Edgerton 1992 Trust); New England Aquarium 46a, 46b; Old South Meeting House 40a; Old Town Trolley Tours 19.
All remaining pictures are held in the Association's own Library (AA Photo Library) and were taken by Clive Sawyer with the exception of the following: R. Holmes, 5b, 13a, 22a, 33b, 36b, 40b, 45b, 49b, 52b, 61a, 87a, 87b; M. Lynch 1, 24b, 25b, 36a, 60, 61b.
Cover Photographs: Main Picture & inset a AA Photo Library (R. Holmes), inset b AA Photo Library (C. Sawyer)

SECOND EDITION UPDATED BY *Sue Gordon and Carolyn Heller*   INDEXER *Marie Lorimer*

Titles in the CityPack series
- Amsterdam • Atlanta • Bangkok • Barcelona • Beijing • Berlin • Boston •
- Brussels & Bruges • Chicago • Dublin • Florence • Hong Kong • Istanbul •
- Lisbon • London • Los Angeles • Madrid • Miami • Montréal • Moscow •
- Munich • New York • Paris • Prague • Rome • San Francisco • Seattle •
- Shanghai • Singapore • Sydney • Tokyo • Toronto • Venice • Vienna •
- Washington •